THE MEANING OF IRONY

SUNY Series, The Margins of Literature
Mihai I. Spariosu, Editor

THE MEANING
OF IRONY

A Psychoanalytic
Investigation

FRANK STRINGFELLOW, JR.

State University
of New York
Press

Published by
State University of New York Press, Albany

© 1994   State University of New York

For information, address State University of New York Press,
State University Plaza, Albany, N.Y., 12246

Production by Susan Geraghty
Marketing by Theresa Abad Swierzowski

Library of Congress Cataloging-in-Publication Data

Stringfellow, Frank, 1948–
     The meaning of irony : a psychoanalytic investigation / by Frank
Stringfellow, Jr.
          p.   cm.
     Includes bibliographical references and index.
     ISBN 0–7914–1977–0 (alk. paper). — ISBN 0–7914–1978–9 (pbk. :
alk. paper)
     1. Irony in literature. 2. Psychoanalysis and literature.
     I. Title.
⌐ PN56.I65S77   1994
     809'.918—dc20   93–35583
                                                                CIP

10 9 8 7 6 5 4 3 2 1

For Tassie and Nick

CONTENTS

ACKNOWLEDGMENTS

Considering how much support, encouragement, and patience others have shown me while I was writing this book, it probably ought to be as monumental as the Encylopedia of Tlön. It is considerably more modest than that, but I hope those mentioned here will nonetheless recognize how grateful I am for their help.

W. Wolfgang Holdheim, having taught me about hermeneutics and many other things, allowed me to find my own way in a different kind of hermeneutic enterprise; to him and to Eva Holdheim, my thanks. William J. Kennedy gave me encouragement at times when it was much appreciated; and at his urging, I have tried to be fairer to the achievements of the rhetorical tradition than I was in earlier drafts. Mihai Spariosu, editor of the series in which this volume appears, was a sympathetic and perceptive reader and offered some essential suggestions that I have heeded as best I could. Carola Sautter, editor at SUNY Press, has provided sane and helpful guidance; I also thank Susan Geraghty, who produced the book, and Ms. Sautter's assistant, Cari Janice. I am grateful as well to Thomas Roberts, archivist for Sigmund Freud Copyrights, who kindly supplied a reference I had not been able to track down, and to Irene T. Soffer, Trustee, Theodor Reik Literary Trust. Dan Sperber, Deirdre Wilson, and Dr. Jorge E. García Badaracco responded generously to my requests for permission to reprint excerpts from their work.

At the University of Miami, I have benefited from the support and encouragement of Zack Bowen (chair par excellence), Patrick McCarthy, Lindsey Tucker, and Peter Bellis, as well as of my former colleagues Hermione de Almeida and George Gilpin. The advice and loyal assistance I have received from Frank Palmeri and Mihoko Suzuki have been invaluable. I appreciate, too, the help of the English Department staff, especially Mary Hope Anderson and Mary Dulik.

My oldest debt of gratitude is to my mother and father, who have supported me in countless ways, material and spiritual, over the years; even in scholarly work—far from their own fields of endeavor—they continue to serve as models for me. I thank as well Elizabeth Ward, William Stringfellow, Kathleen Stringfellow, Stuart Carter, Carter Burns, and Frank and Marjorie Gwilliam for their unfailing interest and encouragement. Whatever I do bears the stamp of my wife Tassie Gwilliam and of the joy she has brought me; her more concrete acts of assistance, even as she was completing her own book, have made this one possible. I dedicate the book to her in thanks for ten wonderful years and to our son Nicholas Gwilliam Stringfellow, who has delighted us beyond measure; the two of them have made everything seem especially worth doing.

A section of chapter 3 is adapted from my essay "Irony and Ideals in *Gulliver's Travels*," in *Critical Essays on Jonathan Swift*, edited by Frank Palmeri. Copyright © 1993 by Frank Palmeri. Used by permission of G. K. Hall & Co., an imprint of Macmillan Publishing Company.

In addition, I gratefully acknowledge permission to reprint the following:

Excerpts from *Dearest Father: Stories and Other Writings* by Franz Kafka, translated by Ernst Kaiser and Eithne Wilkins. English translation copyright © 1954 and renewed 1982 by Schocken Books Inc. Reprinted by permission of Schocken Books, published by Pantheon Books, a division of Random House, Inc.

Excerpts from *The Trial, Definitive Edition* by Franz Kafka, translated by Willa and Edwin Muir, revised by E. M. Butler. Copyright © 1937, 1956 and renewed 1965 by Alfred A. Knopf, Inc. Reprinted by permission of Alfred A. Knopf, Inc. Published in the British Commonwealth by Secker and Warburg Ltd. Reprinted by permission of Secker and Warburg Ltd.

Caption of a drawing by Ed Arno; © 1987 The New Yorker Magazine, Inc. Reprinted by special permission.

Letter from Sigmund Freud to Theodor Reik, dated October 3, 1938. Reprinted by permission of A. W. Freud et al., by arrangement with Mark Paterson & Associates.

An excerpt from Jorge Luis Borges, "Avatars of the Tortoise," in *Labyrinths: Selected Stories and Other Writings*, by Jorge Luis

Borges, edited by Donald A. Yates and James E. Irby, augmented edition (New York: New Directions Publishing Corporation, 1964). Reprinted by permission of New Directions Publishing Corporation.

Excerpts from Franz Kafka, *Der Process*, edited by Malcolm Pasley (Frankfurt am Main: S. Fischer Verlag, 1990), copyright © 1990 by Schocken Books Inc., New York City. Reprinted by permission of S. Fischer Verlag.

Excerpts from Franz Kafka, *Nachgelassene Schriften und Fragmente*, vol. 2, edited by Jost Schillemeit (Frankfurt am Main: S. Fischer Verlag, 1992), copyright © 1992 by Schocken Books Inc., New York City. Reprinted by permission of S. Fischer Verlag.

Excerpts from the *Journal of the Kafka Society of America*, the *Romanic Review,* and *Twentieth Century Literature* appear by permission of the editors of those journals; from the *Journal of Criminal Psychopathology*, by permission of the publisher of *Psychiatry Digest*; from *Psychoanalytic Review*, by permission of The Guilford Press; and from *Psychotherapy and Psychosomatics*, by permission of S. Karger AG, Basel, Switzerland.

Excerpts from Jorge E. García Badaracco, "Identification and Its Vicissitudes in the Psychoses: The Importance of the Concept of the 'Maddening Object,'" *International Journal of Psycho-Analysis* 67 (1986): 133–46, are reprinted by permission of the author and the *International Journal of Psycho-Analysis*.

Excerpts from Dan Sperber and Deirdre Wilson, "Irony and the Use–Mention distinction," *Radical Pragmatics,* edited by Peter Cole (New York: Academic Press, 1981), 295–318, appear by permission of the authors and Academic Press.

CHAPTER 1

Irony and Psychoanalytic Theory

Irony, Freud said, "can be understood without any need for bringing in the unconscious."[1] In accord with this opinion, Freud did
not devote much attention to irony in his psychological writings,
and it receives only two brief discussions in his entire corpus, both
occurring in *Jokes and Their Relation to the Unconscious.*[2] Irony,
therefore, never became a category in the psychoanalytic literature, and it has been passed over by most of Freud's successors,
with the notable exceptions of Theodor Reik and Edmund
Bergler.

This result ought to surprise us. For irony, in the sense of what
is often called "verbal irony," occurs as a phenomenon of everyday behavior; and in psychoanalytic doctrine no human behavior
exists solely in the plane of light, free from the influence of the
unconscious. Some people, indeed, resort to irony characteristi-
cally, invariably, even neurotically; we have all encountered the
person who is not free *not* to speak ironically. It is in such individuals that we see how deeply rooted irony can be in character and,
therefore, how intimate the connection is between irony and the
unconscious determinants of character. Among these individuals
we must surely list some of our greatest writers: Swift, Austen,
Borges, Gogol, Hoffmann.

Why did Freud ignore the unconscious roots of irony? To
answer this question, let us look at the major part of Freud's discussion of irony:

> Its essence lies in saying the opposite of what one intends to
> convey to the other person, but in sparing him contradiction by
> making him understand—by one's tone of voice, by some
> accompanying gesture, or (where writing is concerned) by some
> small stylistic indications—that one means the opposite of what
> one says. Irony can only be employed when the other person is
> prepared to hear the opposite, so that he cannot fail to feel an
> inclination to contradict. As a result of this condition, irony is

exposed particularly easily to the danger of being misunderstood. It brings the person who uses it the advantage of enabling
him readily to evade the difficulties of direct expression, for
instance in invective. It produces comic pleasure in the hearer,
probably because it stirs him into a contradictory expenditure
of energy which is at once recognized as being unnecessary.[3]

What emerges from this passage is that Freud takes an essentially
rhetorical view of irony—naturally enough, since the very concept
comes to us from the rhetorical tradition. Freud treats irony here
exactly as a traditional rhetorician might: it appears as a rationally chosen technique by which a speaker attempts to communi-
cate an intended message to a particular audience. To the question
of why choose a fancy, roundabout means of expression—one
that is "marked," to use the linguistic term—Freud also gives a
traditional answer. Essentially the speaker gains two advantages
by using irony. From her own point of view, she is able "readily to
evade the difficulties of direct expression, for instance in invec-
tives." The difficulties Freud is speaking of here seem to be external—"real"—ones, such as those arising from political censorship. And although in one of his most famous metaphors Freud
compares political censorship and the barrier erected by the ego
to keep unacceptable thoughts from consciousness,[4] here Freud
refuses any comparison between difficulties that might arise
because of the speaker's real external situation and those that
might be posed by the ego's own internal defense system—which,
in its effort to repress or disavow "dangerous" ideas, will seek to
deny them any kind of direct, overt expression. Freud could have
followed such a path into the unconscious of the ironist, but he
did not; this is, of course, precisely the approach we will try to
take. As for the second advantage Freud attributes to the use of
irony—its pleasurable effect on the auditor—Freud restates the
traditional idea that a speaker uses irony, among other available
rhetorical devices, to make what he says more striking, more
memorable; but Freud unpacks this commonplace by speculating
on the exact psychological mechanism by which irony achieves its
pleasurable effect on the auditor.

     If even Freud himself was not able to move from a rhetorical
to a truly psychoanalytic understanding of irony, then we can
understand how powerfully the rhetorical model dominates our
idea of this phenomenon. Certainly this dominance has been evi-

dent in literary studies, as we can see from two of the standard works on irony published in the last twenty-five years, D. C. Muecke's *The Compass of Irony* and Wayne C. Booth's *A Rhetoric of Irony*. Booth's point of view is evident from the title he has chosen, and he makes explicit that he is "attempting only a rhetoric of irony—not a psychology or sociology or metaphysics or ethics of irony."[5] Working within the rhetorical model, a critic may deal with both the speaker and the auditor (and indeed, with any of the other components of linguistic communication, such as code, message, contact, or context—to list the four that Jakobson adds to "addresser" and "addressee"),[6] and we see that Freud, for example, in the passage just quoted focuses on both the producer and the consumer of irony. Booth, however, turns his particular attention to the audience: he especially wants to investigate how the reader knows that an utterance is ironic and how the reader finds her way back to the speaker's intended meaning that lies behind the rhetorical cover. Indeed, in many ways, Booth's work is a semiotic investigation of "code," and as such it remains relatively uninterested in the producer of irony—who would, of course, tend to be the focus of a psychoanalytic investigation.

Muecke's book is more wide ranging, but when he takes up verbal irony, he, too, stays within a rhetorical perspective: "Verbal Irony implies an ironist, someone consciously and intentionally employing a technique," he says, and adds that "talking about Verbal Irony means talking about the ironist's techniques and strategies."[7] Muecke also gives an essentially rhetorical view when he explains why someone might resort to irony in the first place:

> Irony may be used as a rhetorical device to enforce one's meaning. It may be used . . . as a satiric device to attack a point of view or to expose folly, hypocrisy, or vanity. It may be used as an heuristic device to lead one's readers to see that things are not so simple or certain as they seem, or perhaps not so complex or doubtful as they seem. It is probable that most irony is rhetorical, satirical, or heuristic.[8]

The rhetorical model on which Muecke and Booth base their discussions of irony is, it goes without saying, fruitful in a great many ways; but it also obscures important aspects of verbal irony. The reason is evident enough. In this rhetorical model, an ironic utterance is essentially viewed as the transformation of another, more primary statement. The irony is a kind of added step—a

technique or strategy—by which the "original" statement is con-
verted into its negative or (in more artful forms of irony) into
some statement that more or less contradicts the original meaning. But this assumption about verbal irony, implicit in the traditional rhetorical model, contradicts an important aspect of irony
as we encounter it in everyday speech. Most ironic utterances—I
would venture to say—strike us not as a transformation of
another remark but rather as original or primary utterances that
also admit of a secondary and contradictory interpretation and,
indeed, insist that we focus on this secondary interpretation. To
be sure, in analyzing irony, one is naturally tempted to assume
that the production and the reception of irony are two mirror-
image processes—much as the cryptographic encoding and
decoding of a pregiven message (to use a metaphor from some linguistic models) appear as symmetrically reversed procedures.
Such a model helps us to deal with the contradictoriness of verbal
irony by breaking it into two distinct moments; and of course
such a model might be necessary if one actually wanted to demonstrate to another person how to produce an ironic statement. But
(except perhaps in the most obvious sarcasms) do we not sense, in
encountering verbal irony, that the contradictoriness, often so difficult to analyze neatly into its components, has existed from the
very moment of inception of the ironic utterance? If we do, then
we cannot be satisfied with a rhetorical model that views irony as
a kind of secondary transformation; such a model will have
missed the true origin of irony.

The rhetorical model, after all, is not constructed so as to
account for contradictory human intentions. It assumes on the
part of the speaker a pregiven intention (or a set of prereconciled
intentions) that the speaker then carries out by means of certain
linguistic and rhetorical operations. Thus, a rhetorical phenomenon like verbal irony must be analyzed in such a way that it correlates with some form of unitary intention, and if irony seems to
produce two more or less contradictory meanings (and thus intentions), then the meanings must be separated into two different
moments and placed in some kind of hierarchy, so that one intention is clearly primary and the other ultimately derivable from the
primary one. The speaker cannot have started out (i.e., entered
into the rhetorical model) with self-contradictory intentions.

One obvious result of this kind of analysis is that a speaker
cannot "really mean" everything that she is saying. The literal

level of the ironic statement must be explained away as a transformation of the original, underlying utterance, so that one of the meanings that actually emerges from the ironic statement must be subsequently denied as constituting an intended meaning of the utterance. Psychoanalysis invariably takes a quite different point of view. By appealing to the unconscious, it finds meaning even where no consciously intended meaning is evident. And indeed, its suspicions are particularly aroused when the existence of intended meaning is denied with respect to anything that a human being says or does. So the very fact that in encountering irony, in trying to resolve the confusion it presents us with, we tend to look through the surface meaning, as if we were trying to render it transparent—this very fact, which indeed is reflected in the rhetorical model of irony, will make the psychoanalytically minded critic insist all the more that this surface or literal meaning is just as much intended by the ironist as is the meaning "concealed" by the irony. By assuming that a person means everything that she says, psychoanalysis can stay open to meanings that tend to be lost in a rhetorical analysis.

Psychoanalysis, moreover, in dealing with the contradictory intentions represented by the opposed meanings of an ironic statement, does not need to rationalize them into some unitary intention, with the various distortions that such a rationalization is bound to entail. On the contrary, psychoanalysis insists that human phenomena are invariably the product of contradictory impulses and that careful analysis of the product will reveal the opposing elements that entered into its making. Irony is obviously a phenomenon that exhibits contradictory elements in its makeup, and one could suppose that it would best be served by a method of analysis that expects and can account for such contradictoriness.

As a final reason for turning from a rhetorical to a psychoanalytic view of irony, we can surely suppose that if indeed verbal irony appears in some human beings as a deep-rooted, characteristic mode of behavior, then the purposes it serves can in no way be limited to traditional rhetorical ones like those exemplified in the above passages by Muecke and even by Freud. Those purposes are realistically oriented toward the audience of the ironic statement, but there are doubtless other purposes that are aimed not at the ironist's real environment but rather at internal conflicts that the ironist wishes somehow to solve. Psychoanalysis, with its powerful analytic concept of the unconscious, can help us better understand the genesis and meaning of verbal irony by exposing those other, internal purposes that irony is meant to serve.

So long as rhetoric assumes an essentially linguistic model of communication, it is bound to ignore those aspects of ironic speech that result, at least in part, from unconscious motives having little to do with rational purposes of communication. This limitation would certainly characterize, for example, Paolo Valesio's attempt to rethink the theory of rhetoric, because he essentially views rhetoric as the science that describes the "functional, discursive structure" of any utterance and, therefore, as a kind of higher-order linguistics (or as a component of "general linguistics").[9] There may, of course, be other ways to conceive rhetoric. For example, the term sometimes seems to refer simply to a study of tropes and figures, in which case the traditional "rhetorical" approach (based on the model of a speaker trying to persuade an audience) might be only one of several approaches actually brought to bear on the subject.

The work of Group μ (Jacques Dubois et al.) could be assimilated to a rhetoric defined in this manner; and indeed, among theoreticians of rhetoric, the members of Group μ have been the most successful in avoiding the difficulties that I have claimed inhere in a rhetorical approach to irony. For example, in their discussion of irony and related tropes, they bring up the Freudian concept of 'negation' (whereby, for instance, a patient says *sua sponte*, "Of course, I don't hate my father," but unconsciously means that he *does* hate his father—the negation being irrelevant to the unconscious, while serving to disguise the unconscious meaning from the patient's conscious awareness); and indeed, they posit the existence of "a rhetoric of the unconscious," "a rhetoric that escapes the speaker."[10] Yet other than to classify Freudian negation with irony, the members of Group μ do not try to explain what inherent, causal connections these two phenomena might have, nor do they otherwise exploit their insight.

This same stopping short can also be seen in a later work by the same group in which they take a critical commonplace about metaphor and perceptively transfer it to irony as well. The commonplace, in Paul Ricoeur's elegant and uncommon formulation, is that "the impossible literal interpretation is not simply abolished by the metaphorical interpretation but submits to it while resisting."[11] Of irony, Group μ writes: "Let us make clear first of all that the encoder, when he states *x*, does not give up the idea of making us understand *x* as well as *not-x*. To neglect this polysemous intention, this wish to assume two isotopies at the same time, would lead us to confuse rhetoric and simple transcoding (with a cryptographic function, for example) and to fall back into the idea that the 'figurative sense' is only an ornamental translation of the 'proper sense.'"[12] This point has more readily been made about metaphor than about irony because we are not particularly troubled by the idea that a statement can mean two different (but not contradictory) things. Group μ takes the next step, and yet the authors don't fully acknowledge the radicalness of their move—as if it doesn't matter whether "polysemous" refers to merely different or to contradictory meanings. As with traditional rhetorical models, they simply accept as a given the intention with which a speaker enters the rhetorical situation, even when they imply that this "intention" can be two contradictory intentions. They critique the model of coding and decoding, and yet the language of that model is still the language they use.

Several recent discussions of irony within the field of linguistics (or within the neighboring field of the philosophy of language) have attempted to extend the analysis of irony offered by rhetoric proper, and in some cases they have produced notable insights. But as with rhetorical analyses that rely on an essentially linguistic model of communication, linguistics ultimately butts up against the limitations of its methods and assumptions: in focusing on communication, which at least in the ideal requires univocal meaning, linguistics looks past any ambivalence on the part of the speaker—although, as I hope to make clear, this ambivalence has tremendous influence on the linguistic product we designate as irony.

Of these linguistic discussions, two stand out. The first is a 1981 article by Dan Sperber and Deirdre Wilson, "Irony and the Use-Mention Distinction."[13] Sperber and Wilson recall the logical distinction between "use" and "mention" ("USE of an expression involves reference to what the expression refers to; MENTION of an expression involves reference to the expression itself" [303]) and then argue that an ironical proposition is not actually being "used" by the speaker but only "mentioned." Ironical utterances, therefore, are "semantically distinguishable from cases where the same proposition is used in order to make an assertion, ask a question, and so on" (316). Of course, what makes these cases of mention *ironical* is the fact that they "are interpreted as echoing a remark or opinion that the speaker wants to characterize as ludicrously inappropriate or irrelevant" (310).

At the simplest level, mention is indicated in writing by the use of quotation marks: if I want to refer to a word *as a word*—and not to the thing it stands for—I can put it in quotation marks (e.g., if I wanted to discuss the history of the word "irony"); or if I want to refer to an entire statement that someone else has made, and at the same time wish to make clear that I am not myself making this statement, I can put it in quotation marks, generally with a "he said" tag of some kind. Sperber and Wilson claim that irony involves precisely this kind of mention, except that the mention is generally implicit rather than explicit; in other words, it is not accompanied by any formal sign that the statement is being mentioned rather than used. According to their theory, the following exchange from *Pride and Prejudice*, cited by the authors, would be paradigmatic of all irony; the speakers here are Darcy and Elizabeth Bennet:

> "You take an eager interest in that gentleman's concerns," said Darcy in a less tranquil tone, and with a heightened colour.
> "Who that knows what his misfortunes have been, can help feeling an interest in him?"
> "His misfortunes!" repeated Darcy contemptuously; "yes, his misfortunes have been great indeed."[14]

Sperber and Wilson do not, of course, believe that all examples of irony involve so obvious a case of mention; as they explain, "some are immediate echoes, and others delayed; some have their source in actual utterances, others in thoughts and opinions; some have a real source, others an imagined one; some are traceable back to a particular individual, whereas others have a vaguer origin" (309–10).

The insight that the ironist is echoing the words or thoughts of another person is an exceptionally fruitful one, and in fact, it was enunciated many years ago by the analyst Theodor Reik. But the linguistic version of this insight, as Sperber and Wilson expound it, is deficient in at least one regard. If I wanted to "mention" someone else's words (in order to indicate that I find them irrelevant, inappropriate, or foolish), why would I resort to *implicit* rather than explicit mention? Why would I leave ambiguous the issue of whether I was actually using the proposition or simply mentioning it? This is the problem that Sperber and Wilson's theory cannot really deal with. The problem can be seen in a particularly interesting form in literary irony that is associated with free indirect discourse, as literary irony often is. Sperber and Wilson claim that their theory will help to explain this association, since free indirect discourse involves precisely the mention of another person's words or thoughts. But again, the authors ignore a critical aspect of their example, that in free indirect discourse the author purposely obscures the fact that the narrative utterance does not really belong to the narrator.

Sperber and Wilson are attempting to evade the logical difficulties that arise when we say that a statement either figuratively means, or else conversationally implicates (to use the formulation of H. P. Grice),[15] the opposite of what it literally says. But ultimately they resort to the same maneuver that rhetoric has always used in trying to solve this problem: the ironist does not really mean what she is saying—she is, in Sperber and Wilson's formulation, only "mentioning" the proposition. Yet the very fact that irony is so often misunderstood suggests that ironists themselves do not always issue an unambiguous disclaimer. The question is, why not? And unless one simply wants to remain with the practical response that ironists are trying to say what could not be said publicly, only psychoanalysis can satisfactorily deal with this question.[16]

The linguist whose work on irony shows the most subtle appreciation of its nuances, probably because of her attention to the literal level of the ironic statement, is Catherine Kerbrat-Orecchioni; and her two articles on irony constitute the other important linguistic discussion that requires some comment here.[17] Kerbrat-Orecchioni, for example, recognizes more fully than do Sperber and Wilson and most traditional analyses that "ambiguity is distinctively constitutive of irony."[18] And in expanding this point, she takes a position reminiscent of Group μ's: "That is why an ironic sequence is never equivalent to its literal translation. In this regard, irony is related to the trope, whose smooth functioning implies, similarly, the recognition of two superposed semantic levels, neither of which must obscure the other."[19] Unfortunately, in trying to account for the fact that "irony is justified only to the extent that it remains at least partially ambiguous," Kerbrat-Orecchioni resorts to a bland rhetorical explanation: "what advantage would there be in speaking ironically if we are only going to immediately correct the range and specify what we *really* want to say?"[20]

Nevertheless, by insisting that the literal level of an ironic statement does not simply disappear, Kerbrat-Orecchioni is able to pay more attention to it than it usually receives. She notes, for example, that irony effects "a reversal of the usual hierarchy of semantic levels: as soon as it is identified, the derived value finds itself promoted to the rank of denotative value, while the literal sense finds itself degraded in the form of a connoted trace."[21] And she observes an interesting aspect of the literal level in "citational irony" (she believes that only some cases of irony involve the echoic mention that Sperber and Wilson find typical of all irony): just as irony often allows the ironist to evade moral or political censure and say things that can not be said openly, "in citational irony we can see a similar transgressive aspect, except that here it is the literal sense, and not the insinuated sense, which for the speaker is affected by a certain taboo: the perverse pleasure of using a feint to appropriate words that at the same time one violently impugns, and thereby of being able to say things that one forbids oneself from saying."[22] It must be added, however, that Kerbrat-Orecchioni does not develop either of these significant insights in any systematic way; as is particularly evident in the case of the second observation (but as we will see, is also true of the first), she would need a psychological framework in order to do so.

It is precisely this shift in framework that the present study will undertake. Obviously, it cannot do without the insights of rhetoric and linguistics—on the contrary. But it will attempt to demonstrate that only by bringing in the findings, and indeed the fundamental point of view, of psychoanalysis can we reach a fully adequate understanding of verbal irony.

In speaking about irony, we have so far been using the term to describe a phenomenon that is often labeled more narrowly as "verbal irony" or "rhetorical irony." If we consider the history of the term *irony*, we will see why, for the purposes of the present investigation, it is necessary to restrict our use of the term to this most traditional meaning and to leave out of consideration some of the extensions that the term has undergone during the last two centuries.

From at least the writings of Quintilian until around the middle of the eighteenth century, the term *irony* seems to have been used in Europe in predominantly one basic sense: saying the opposite of what one means, usually in order to blame through praise or to praise through blame.[23] Quintilian, for example, in his most extended discussion of irony, says that in irony "contrarium ei quod dicitur intelligendum est" [we understand something which is the opposite of what is actually said].[24] This sense of the word *irony* persists in major European languages such as English, German, French, and Russian, though it is now joined by a number of other meanings as well.[25] We may think of it as the basic rhetorical sense of the concept.[26]

Beginning in the latter part of the eighteenth century, however, this basic sense was extended in a number of different directions. The German romantics, especially, went far beyond any rhetorical definition, relying in part on the Greek use of the term *eirōneia* to describe Socrates' pretense of ignorance in the dialogues (a use that is actually older than the rhetorical sense of the word). Friedrich Schlegel, in one of his *Lyceum* fragments, writes:

> Die Philosophie ist die eigentliche Heimat der Ironie, welche man logische Schönheit definieren möchte . . . Freilich gibts auch eine rhetorische Ironie, welche sparsam gebraucht vortreffliche Wirking tut, besonders im Polemischen; doch ist sie gegen die erhabne Urbanität der sokratischen Muse, was die Pracht der glänzendsten Kunstrede gegen eine alte Tragödie in hohem Styl.
>
> [Philosophy is the true home of irony, which might be defined as logical beauty . . . It is true, there is also a rhetorical irony which, if sparingly used, performs a very excellent function, especially in polemics, but compared to the lofty urbanity of the Socratic muse, rhetorical irony is like the splendor of the most brilliant oratory compared to ancient high tragedy.][27]

As this passage illustrates, irony in Schlegel's hands could easily be made to exceed its rhetorical brief and to become instead a more highly charged, but much vaguer, term of general approbation ("logical beauty"). This trend has continued into our own century, for example, in the New Critical use of the term *irony*, and thus we find Cleanth Brooks claiming that "irony is our most general term for indicating that recognition of incongruities— which, again, pervades all poetry to a degree far beyond what our conventional criticism has been heretofore willing to allow."[28]

In *The Concept of Irony*, Kierkegaard joined Schlegel in rejecting a merely rhetorical understanding of irony, but he extended the term in a somewhat different, and much more specific, direction than did Schlegel. In discussing the *Phaedo*, for example, Kierkegaard tells us that the "ironic ornamentations scattered throughout the dialogue . . . are able to be at most only a hint of the ultimate view that permeates the entire dialogue,"[29] and it is this ultimate view—rather than the "ornamentations" (i.e., the concrete instances of irony)—that Kierkegaard wishes to define as irony in the true sense, or as he calls it, irony "*sensu eminentiori*" (254). At this most fundamental level, irony "is directed not against this or that particular existing entity but against the entire given actuality at a certain time and under certain conditions" (254). Irony becomes a kind of existential stance or position, which Kierkegaard—picking up on a suggestion by Hegel—labels as "infinite absolute negativity" (254). The advantage to the ironist is freedom: "In irony, the subject is continually retreating, talking every phenomenon out of its reality in order to save itself—that is, in order to preserve itself in negative independence of everything" (257).

Unlike Schlegel and his New Critical descendants, Kierkegaard does not regard irony as the highest value. He is enough of a Hegelian to believe in a higher stage, in this case one in which irony is controlled or mastered and the ironist achieves a new relation to actuality; "what doubt is to science," Kierkegaard writes, "irony is to personal life" (326).

For all of its suggestiveness, Kierkegaard's philosophical elaboration of the "concept" of irony has severe limitations. The main problem is that in focusing on irony as negativity, he flattens out the doubleness that is surely the most salient and characteristic feature of irony. Thus, for example, he downplays the importance of dissimulation in irony (255–56); he is much more interested in the subjective pleasure that the ironist derives from her negative freedom than he is in the veiled and apparently contradictory manner in which she "asserts" this freedom. Indeed, Kierkegaard denies any real significance to the specifically ironic aspect of an ironic statement: "The ironic figure of speech cancels itself . . . inasmuch as the one who is speaking assumes that his hearers understand him" (248). This is a good observation, of course, insofar as it highlights the problem with the traditional understanding of rhetorical irony—the problem of explaining why someone would bother to use irony in the first place. But even if logic seems to suggest that the ironic statement cancels itself out, surely our intuition suggests that something remains; and the point is to investigate exactly what this remnant is.[30]

In addition to the kinds of philosophical extension that may be seen in the work of Schlegel, Kierkegaard, and others, the term *irony* has also been much extended through various analogical developments; here we might place such terms as *dramatic irony* or the *irony of fate* (the latter of which lies behind the the popular usage: "it's ironic that . . ."). And as a result of both the philosophical and the analogical extensions, more than one critic has concluded, to quote Jonathan Tittler: "Irony has meant and means so many different things to different people that rarely is there a meeting of minds as to its particular sense on a given occasion."[31] There have, of course, been attempts to reintroduce a unified definition, as well as to enumerate the various senses that have been employed. Muecke's attempt at a definition—the most successful, in my view—is instructive:

> In the first place irony is a double-layered or two-storey phenomenon . . . In the second place there is always some kind of opposition between the two levels, an opposition that may take the form of contradiction, incongruity, or incompatibility . . . In the third place there is in irony an element of "innocence" . . . [32]

Muecke has been able to generalize a definition from the various uses of the term *irony* by removing the personal subject from his formulation—an effect that I have exaggerated by quoting only the first part of each of his three "essential elements" of irony. But if, in this investigation, we are going to look at irony as a form of behavior that can be analyzed in psychoanalytic terms, then we will need to put the personal subject back so that we can have an actor, an ironist to go with the ironic behavior. And when we put the ironist back into Muecke's formulation, we see that, essentially, we are back to the rhetorical model of irony (with the useful addition of the requirement that the ironist be, or pretend to be, innocent)—from which Muecke obviously had to abstract in the first place.

In other words, not only is verbal irony—the irony of the rhetorical tradition—the *historical* point of departure for various other definitions of irony, but it remains the conceptual model for them as well. It therefore has a certain claim to being the focus of any investigation of irony. In addition, as compared to the analogical extensions of the term *irony,* verbal irony gives us by far the best chance to relate the phenomenon of irony to some concrete ironist (human ironist, I should say, given the concept of the 'irony of fate'). Only the philosophical extensions of the term offer a similar opportunity, but here too, for the purposes of this study, there are reasons for preferring a focus on verbal irony. For one thing, verbal irony is much easier to identify than are the more philosophical brands of irony, and therefore it is much easier to treat as a discrete, analyzable phenomenon of behavior. If the philosophical conceptions of irony actually stand for the cumulative effect of numerous smaller ironies, then we might as well start with an analysis of the smaller units, presumably the concrete verbal ironies. If they don't, if they refer instead to some kind of irreducible, overall view of life and art—as both Schlegel's and Kierkegaard's conceptions of irony seem to do—then we may find it hard to agree on what exactly characterizes this view; one example of this difficulty would be Kierkegaard's questionable focus on negativity rather than on doubleness in his account of irony (in his conception, irony is closer to doubt than, say, to lying). Then, too, in some philosophical conceptions irony becomes a kind of accolade that would apply so broadly—to all great writers, for example—that we would hardly know what it is we were trying to study (creativity, perhaps). Insofar as we are treating irony as a form of verbal behavior, we would surely do better to avoid the vaguer philosophical conceptions and restrict ourselves to the more carefully delimited phenomenon of verbal irony.

In addition to settling on a definition of irony to be used in the present study, we need to consider briefly the relation between irony as it appears in literature and irony that is used in ordinary speech. In the simplest case, such as the Austen passage given above, where literary dialogue simply imitates the irony of everyday speech, there is obviously no need to make a distinction. And even in more complicated instances, we will take the position here that there is no essential difference between ironic statements that occur in the two contexts. There are, however, heuristic reasons for focusing first on one context and then on the other.

In some respects, literary irony might seem to offer a clearer model for analysis. All verbal irony demands a split in the way that the speaker represents himself, but in literature this split often seems to be reified in the distinction we make between author and character: in an ironic statement, the character means one thing and the author means something else. As we will see, however, the state of affairs is actually more complicated than this model would suggest. Indeed, since our approach demands that irony be related to a concrete ironist, as soon as we look at irony in literature we are immediately involved in the intricate and theoretically difficult problem of how the mediations—and pseudomediations—of fictional characters and fictional authors affect the relationship between author and work. (Muecke catches this problem nicely when he writes, "There are . . . difficult cases, as in the *Canterbury Tales* for example, where we never know when the author is ironically feigning naïveté or when he is interposing between himself and us a naïve, ironized narrator."[33]) In addition, the question of treating all or part of a literary work as the verbal behavior of an author is so vexed that we must approach it in as cautious and well prepared a manner as possible. In these respects, we would do better to tackle the complexities of literary examples only after we have developed concepts and frames of reference based on simpler, "everyday" examples of verbal irony. I therefore begin, in the next section, with three instances of ordinary verbal irony (one perhaps controversially so) that will serve as paradigms for our analysis of irony.

On the other hand, the ultimate focus of this study will be on literary irony, for there is much that this kind of irony can teach us about the phenomenon of irony generally. The rich fantasies, conscious and unconscious, out of which all literary works are elaborated provide an abundance of information about the mind that has created the literary work; and if we proceed tactfully, we can usefully correlate the fantasies to be found in a work and the verbal irony that is a similar emanation of the mind of the author and that results, at least in part, from similar unconscious determinants. This procedure must find its justification in the insights it provides; I do, however, attempt some theoretical justification for it in chapter 2.

As for the particular literary works to be considered, I have chosen two: Jonathan Swift's *Gulliver's Travels* and Franz Kafka's *Der Prozess* (*The Trial*). *Gulliver's Travels* is an obvious enough choice in that Swift is the acknowledged supreme master of traditional, rhetorical forms of verbal irony, and *Gulliver's Travels* is widely considered to be his greatest work. But *Gulliver's Travels* is appropriate for another reason, too: it is a work in which the infantile fantasies that help determine its shape are almost completely out in the open—in fact, they force themselves on us. What remains for us to do is to delineate the fantasies carefully and then try to connect them with the verbal irony that is an equally significant feature of the book. Kafka's *Trial*, on the other hand, is here because it is a hard case, a borderline example of the verbal irony we are analyzing; in showing how its irony diverges from the classical model of verbal irony exhibited in *Gulliver's Travels*, and why it might do so, we will attempt to extend the conclusions worked out in the chapter on Swift. Needless to say, *The Trial* is also here because the generality of our analysis of irony is well tested by the obvious differences between a work written by an Anglo-Irish clergyman and published in 1726 and one composed by a Jewish intellectual living in the German and Czech city of Prague in the first quarter of the twentieth century. And yet we will find that the impulse to irony found in *Gulliver's Travels* and *The Trial* correlates with important similarities between the fantasies present in the two books and between the plots in which those fantasies are elaborated.

THREE PARADIGMS OF IRONY

We begin this investigation by analyzing from our particular point of view two fairly ordinary instances of irony and a third example that can be interpreted to represent something that from a rhetorical point of view is impossible—unconscious irony. Here, then, is the first case: You walk into a colleague's office and glance down at the draft of a lecture he is writing; the handwriting looks like chicken scratches. "Why, I didn't know you knew shorthand!" you say.

When we think about what makes a statement ironic, we reach first for the formula, "saying the opposite of what one means." And second, we think of the paradigmatic instance of this reversal: seeming to praise, when one means to blame. Our first case illustrates, roughly, both of these formulas. But notice that your statement is not precisely the opposite of what you mean. If you mean to say, "You have an ugly, illegible handwriting," then the opposite would be a simpler statement than the one you have actually made: "Why, what a beautiful, legible handwriting you have!" Certainly we would also have classified this latter statement as ironic, but we would have labeled it as "sarcastic" as well. What is the relationship between these two categories? When one is speaking sarcastically, then one generally does say exactly the opposite of what one means, and one also leaves absolutely no doubt—not even for the slightest moment—about what one means. On the other hand, ironic statements are usually more artful, in both senses of the word. As in our first example, they do not exist as one of two opposite poles; their exact location on the spectrum that includes, at one end, the "meaning that one actually intended" and, at the other, the opposite of this meaning is somewhat vague. In the second place, ironic statements generally do leave the listener with a momentary confusion about the precise meaning that the speaker intended. As we have seen, Freud emphasized, in his brief discussion of irony, precisely this tendency on the part of the auditor to misinterpret for an instant the speaker's true meaning. So, while we do not want to exclude sarcasm from the realm of irony, we need to see it as a limiting case on the very border of the ironic. It tends to lack that slight indeterminacy with which most ironic statements escape the easy formulation of saying the opposite of what one means.

How, then, *does* our example escape this easy formulation? Primarily by existing on several levels at once, on each one of which the truth value of the statement is somewhat different. Notice, for example, that at the most literal level, the statement you have made to your colleague is perfectly true: You did not know that he knew shorthand, and indeed you *could* not have known it, since—as you are perfectly aware—he doesn't know the first mark in the any shorthand system. But of course, your statement naturally suggests the extension, But I see now that you do know shorthand. This statement—one that is virtually included in the words you actually uttered—is false. But on the level of this statement, you are still not criticizing your colleague or his handwriting. You have credited him with an accomplishment that he does not possess; but on the other hand you do not mean to fault him for not having learned this skill. You have fabricated a lie, a fiction, whose denial would leave you in a zero position. You do not mean the opposite of what you have (virtually) said, and in the present context you would never have bothered to assert the opposite, true statement that, from what you can see, your colleague does not know shorthand. At this level, your statement seems to be a kind of gratuitous fiction that can be denied but whose denial would not really constitute any kind of relevant assertion. Only at a third level do we find a real opposition between what you have said and what we may take you to mean. To get to this level, we need to take your statement one step backwards: I see that you know shorthand because I am looking at your draft and the marks there resemble shorthand strokes. Even at this level, the observation that lies at the heart of your exclamation is absolutely true: the marks on your colleague's draft *do* look like shorthand strokes. But you have drawn the "wrong" conclusion from this observation. The ordinary conclusion would be that your colleague has an illegible handwriting and merits at least some faint disapproval on account of his penmanship. You, however, have chosen a possible, but unlikely, interpretation of the evidence before your eyes. Here, at last, you are saying the opposite of what you mean. Of two possible conclusions you might draw, one would redound to your colleague's credit and the other to his discredit. The conclusions are in a sense opposites, since one logically excludes the other, and you have expressed the one that does not reflect your true opinion.

Notice, then, that this single piece of irony blends fact, fiction, and falsehood. At the deepest level you have spoken falsely: you have implied your belief in an opinion that you do not hold and that you do not expect anyone else to hold either. But you have uttered a statement that a legalist of the word could not indict as false. You have preserved what, in political life, we have learned to call "deniability." And whereas the ordinary observer would think of only one possible conclusion about your colleague's handwriting, you have invented an alternate explanation, a fiction, a possible world—and logically, this alternate explanation has just as much chance of being true as does the commonsense conclusion.

Indeed, suppose that your colleague answers, "Why, yes, as a matter of fact I do know shorthand. I learned it while I was working as a reporter for the *Times* of London. Most English journalists are required to use shorthand, you know." You have been caught in your irony, but you still have a modicum of protection. After all, your literal statement tended to affirm, rather than to deny, that your acquaintance knew shorthand; and he himself cannot actually contradict what you have said at the most literal levels. Your literal meanings have served to defend you against a frontal counterattack, since you can always claim, "What I (literally) said is what I meant." On the other hand, you also have available an even more thoroughgoing defense, one that contradicts this first defense. For if, *in some sense* you did not mean what you said, and if your listener chooses to interpret your remark as if, in this sense, you did not mean what you said, then you can always claim not to have meant what you said in other senses as well: "Oh, I didn't really mean it. Actually, you have a very nice handwriting; it just struck me as unusual, that's all." In other words, once you and your listener have both admitted the principle that you might not have meant exactly what you said, then you may feel free to apply this principle in any way you want.

Both of these contradictory defenses are, of course, absolutely specious. Wayne Booth spends much of his book on the rhetoric of irony demonstrating that, in the case of what he calls "stable irony," we don't have any trouble at all interpreting exactly what the ironist intended to say, and certainly our present example would be an instance of stable irony. Yet as we will see, the presence of these possible defenses, however theoretical, and however specious from the point of view of commonsense linguistic experience, makes up an important part of the psychological structure of irony. At the unconscious level, the ironist is trying to have it both ways—in a manner explained quite clearly by Pechorin, Lermontov's super-self-conscious "hero of our time": "I never disclose my secrets myself, but I am awfully fond of having them divined, because that way I can always repudiate them if necessary."[34]

The last thing to notice about this first example of irony is that, in your exclamation to your colleague, you have presented yourself as a kind of naïf. To some extent, this naïf is aware of his ignorance. He is surprised to learn something that he didn't know, and at the moment of his enlightenment he is even a little surprised at his previous ignorance; he probably should have been aware that his colleague knew shorthand. But of course the naïf is much more benighted than he realizes. He has such a simple, unquestioning faith in his colleague's potency and accomplishments that he perverts the evidence of his eyes and strains to reach a conclusion that might credit, rather than criticize, his acquaintance. The naïve speaker is, of course, a staple of literary irony; Lemuel Gulliver comes to mind as a prime example. But in literature the naïve speaker ordinarily becomes a character in his or her own right. Even when the naïve speaker is not a well-defined character, as readers we want to distinguish this speaker from the knowing author, and we will do what we can to visualize this speaker as someone different from the author. In the present case, no such easy distinction is possible. In everyday life, we do not ordinarily distinguish different people within a single speaking voice. On the other hand, if we take this everyday instance of irony as paradigmatic, then we can see that literature, when it creates naïve speakers, develops in extreme form a tendency that characterizes irony generally. In the case we are examining, we seemed to have a simple instance of one person using ironic indirection to criticize, to attack if you will, another person. But even here the ironic critique turns out to depend on the speaker's pose of naïveté. This feature, in fact, tends to characterize irony generally.

Why should a person who speaks ironically tend to cast himself as a naïf? Surely considerations of self-defense play a role here, as they did when we looked at the curious mixture of truth and falsehood in an ironic statement. In the present example, the need for defense is obvious—more obvious, indeed, than in most instances of irony. You have attacked your colleague without any mediation except what your irony itself provides. In *The Compass of Irony*, Muecke distinguishes between the "object of irony"— the person or institution that the ironist is actually attacking— and the "victim of irony"—the person who hears or reads the ironic remark and who might conceivably be taken in by it.[35] But in the present case, the object and the victim are the same person, and the object of your attack cannot fail to hear your criticism, unless he misinterprets your irony. There is no three-part structure here, as, for example, Freud discerned in the structure of tendentious jokes. According to Freud, when a person tells a dirty joke, his immediate audience is the innocent bystander who will derive pleasure from it; but for its effect the joke requires also an ultimate, though absent, audience—namely, the woman at whose expense the joke is being told.[36] This three-part structure would certainly be typical of much irony as well, especially literary irony; the person or type of person being attacked might well read an ironic work, but the irony does not depend on anyone's empirical knowledge that this person has actually received the poison-pen letter that the ironist has sent. On the other hand, this person certainly belongs necessarily to the structure of the irony, and in some respects the ironist certainly wants her message to get through to this person. It is this fact that the present case makes clear. Irony can dispense with the innocent bystander; it can show only a two-part structure, consisting of the ironist and the person at whom his irony is directed. It is this person whom the ironist must protect himself from, and it is this necessity that lies at the heart of the irony. The ironist must protect himself because what he wants to say will invite a counterattack.

So the ironist's naïveté is not simply for "rhetorical effect." In reaching for the guise of childlike innocence, the ironist hopes to be accorded some of the child's perquisites, especially the defense of defenselessness and unknowingness. But there is surely a second reason lying behind the ironist's pose of naïveté. For in reducing himself to the level of the child or the naïf—psychologically the two must be seen as equivalent, even though, in the terminology that has grown up around the concept of irony, we usually speak of the naïf—in doing this, the ironist has performed an unflattering operation on himself as well. He has denied his own knowledge and competence, and, whatever psychological gains he hopes to attain thereby, he has still made himself a victim of his own irony, both in Muecke's sense of the word and in a more general sense as well. It is this self-directed quality of irony that we will look at in the second example offered here as a paradigm of irony.

In June, 1938, Theodor Reik, one of Freud's disciples who, like Freud, had had to flee the Nazi regime, emigrated from the Netherlands to the United States. Reik wrote Freud a letter in which, as Reik says, "I again complained about the hostility and indifference of my New York colleagues."[37] In Freud's last letter to Reik, dated October 13, 1938 (Freud was to die the following year), Freud responded to this earlier letter of Reik's:

> Ich bin bereit, Ihnen zu helfen, sobald ich die Nachricht bekommen habe, dass ich, wenn auch nur für kurze Zeit, mit der Machtvollkommenheit des lieben Gottes betraut bin. Bis dahin müssen Sie allein weiter rackern.
>
> [I am ready to help you as soon as I get the news that I am equipped with the omnipotence of God, if only for a short time. Until then, you must continue to toil alone.][38]

How would one feel upon reading such a letter? Chastened certainly, and chastened in the sense of having been punished by the stern disapproval of the authority figure. You complain too much, says Freud. You bother me with things I can't do anything about. You are being childish in attributing to me powers I don't possess and in expecting me to solve your problems for you. So

Freud's ironic comment contains at its core an attack on his disciple Reik, however softened, muffled, or mediated this attack might be; and the attack shows again the two-part structure we noticed in the first example. When we speak of irony in rhetorical terms, we focus on the transformation that takes place between the covert meaning and the overt meaning and on the deciphering that the listener performs in getting back to the covert meaning. However, from a psychological point of view we want to know why this transformation is necessary in the first place, and to answer this question we have to consider the nature of the statement that the speaker feels the need to transform. Our first two examples are typical in this regard: the statement that the speaker wants to disguise is a hostile one; it is an attack on someone, perhaps even on the speaker's immediate audience.

Freud's remark to Reik also gives further evidence that the transformation is no one-to-one mapping of meanings that the speaker actually intends into meanings that he does not intend. Freud says, "I am ready to help you," and insofar as this readiness refers to Freud's willingness and even his desire to help Reik, surely he means exactly what he says. He goes on, however, to qualify his statement: "as soon as I get the news that I am equipped with the omnipotence of God." If this condition is an impossible one, then Freud has in fact negated the first clause of his sentence; if Freud is ready to help Reik only under an impossible condition, then he is not ready to help him at all. Moreover, if Freud denies that he is ready to help in the sense of "able to help," then by a quibble on the two senses of the word *ready* (and the original German word, *bereit,* works the same way), Freud ends up denying that he is ready in the sense of "willing" to aid Reik. Thus, if Freud does not want to get caught in intolerable self-contradiction, then he cannot view the condition as impossible, and one can only conclude that the author of this sentence believes that at some point he will indeed receive news that he is equipped with the omnipotence of God. Of course, we have now reached the point at which we feel compelled to separate Freud the speaker from the "true" Freud; in this one localized part of the ironic statement, Freud the speaker seems to be saying the opposite of what Freud actually believes to be true. Freud presents himself as, again, a kind of naïf who does not yet realize what all adult, rational human beings realize: that never in our lives will any of us receive such a piece of news. But notice that Freud the speaker does not actually *say* that he believes this bit of news will arrive some day. He puts this part of his statement into an open condition. To be sure, *as soon as* is not quite as open as a simple *if*—this conjunction does imply a certain expectation on the part of the speaker that the condition will come true. Nevertheless, the speaker makes no absolute commitment to a belief that Freud does not, in fact, actually share. We can pin the speaker down only by showing him, through logical deduction, that he is in danger of contradicting himself unless he believes that this condition will come to pass—and by insisting that, as a mature adult, he must speak in such a way that he does not contradict himself within the space of a single sentence. But as in the first example, Freud has afforded himself a certain amount of legalistic and literalistic protection.

We must go further. We have said that Freud, as a reasonably normal adult, does not actually believe that he will be greeted with news about being equipped with divine omnipotence. But of course, Freud—as the successor to the child he once was—undoubtedly retained in his unconscious an archaic belief in precisely his own omnipotence; and to *this* Freud, such news would scarcely even come as a surprise. So even in that part of his statement where Freud seems most clearly to be saying the opposite of what he truly believes, Freud has quite possibly expressed one of the most tenacious beliefs that he, or any other human being, can hold.[39] The ironist here can have it both ways: what consciousness (the adult ego) denies, the unconscious affirms. It is therefore impossible in this case for the ironist to say something that he does not at some level believe. Of course, because the speaker here is Freud himself, the situation is a bit more complicated. The founder of psychoanalysis knows perfectly well about the survival of infantile notions of omnipotence. He also knows how little access we have to this unconscious belief, so that consciousness could never truly admit that we believe ourselves to be omnipotent—even if intellectually we conclude that we have such an unconscious belief.

What we are running into here is a particularly complicated instance of the Freudian idea of negation.[40] To Freud, if it occurs to us to deny a particular thought—that is, if a thought occurs to us in its negative form—then the thought is actually one that is held by the unconscious, which knows no negative. This thought is not acceptable to the conscious, and yet it is not so thoroughly

repressed that it cannot reach consciousness in any form whatsoever. The compromise that the unconscious works out with the
censorship is to admit the thought to consciousness by consciously
denying it. Therefore, if it so much as occurs to Freud to deny that
he is omnipotent, then we may take this asseveration as a sign
that, unconsciously, Freud believes himself to be omnipotent. But
when Freud puts the asseveration in ironic form, his unconscious
actually wins a better compromise: he is able to say straight out,
without any literal negation, that he expects to receive news about
his omnipotence. The denial of the statement is left only to be
inferred. Here, then, we see a second major psychological purpose
for putting a statement in ironic form: irony not only allows the
ironist a certain defense, however imaginary, against counterattack but may also allow him to express, in a literally uncensored
form, unconscious beliefs that consciousness would normally
refuse to admit.

Yet Freud, like all ironists, pays a price for these two psychological advantages, and, in the case of each advantage, the price is
directly suited to the gain. This relationship emerges even more
clearly in the present example than in the first paradigm we
looked at above. In the first place, we can see that even though
Freud's ironic remark strikes out at Reik, Freud himself is as
much its victim (in the ordinary sense of the word, rather than in
Muecke's specialized sense) as Reik is. In the first example, we
noted that the ironist turned himself into a naïf, at the expense of
presenting himself as a knowledgeable adult. In the present case,
however, Freud makes a more specific, more substantive attack on
himself. He reminds Reik, and himself, of his own powerless-
ness—at the very end of his life, he pointedly notes that he does
not have the omnipotence of God. Furthermore, he virtually
attacks himself for any presumptions he may have harbored
about his own omnipotence. This kind of self-attack is, of course,
a recurrent feature of irony and, from a psychological point of
view, could be explained in a number of ways. But in these two
examples, as well as in others we might look at, we notice that the
self-attack is intimately associated with the attack on someone
else, and it is this juxtaposition that helps explain what is going
on in the unconscious of the ironist. The self-attack is the price
the ironist pays for his attack on the other. You—the ironist
says—do not need to punish me for my words because I have
already punished myself. Or alternatively, I am allowed to lash

out at you because I am doing the same thing to myself.

Similarly, in Freud's remark to Reik we see the ironist expressing in a literally uncensored form an unconscious belief that the conscious ego would have to repudiate. Yet here again the ironist pays a price. He expresses the belief, but at the same time he ridicules himself for the belief. We might even say that this ridicule—indeed, this public exposure of his secret wish—is a way of punishing himself for holding on to an infantile notion that is no longer acceptable to the adult ego.

From these two examples we begin to see the complex psychological foundation of the kinds of ironic remarks that we hear in everyday speech. It is my contention that the psychological issues raised by these two paradigms are crucial for understanding literary irony as well, but of course literary irony often has an additional complication. For in literature the uncomprehending speaker can be presented as someone different from the author whose true meaning differs from that of this speaker. On the other hand, in the two examples we have examined, the two figures must be seen as the same person: the ironist knows he is being ironic even as he presents himself as a person unaware of his own irony. In order to make the transition between our two everyday examples and the kind of irony we often see in literature, we need to consider the possibility that a speaker engaging in ordinary linguistic behavior might be speaking ironically and not be aware that she is doing so—in other words, the possibility that a speaker might be *unconsciously* ironic. From the point of view of traditional rhetoric such a possibility cannot be admitted, since irony appears in that light as an intentional device for having a certain effect on one's audience. But from a psychological point of view we can at least conceive of the possibility. Consider the following example, the third paradigm we will examine here.

In his *History of English Criminal Law*, Leon Radzinowicz tells us that in late eighteenth-century England the laws often called for capital punishment for criminals convicted of relatively minor offenses (e.g., for stealing goods worth forty shillings or more) but that in practice judges often worked around these harsh laws. In the case of one crime, however, the execution demanded by law tended to be carried out, and this was for the crime of forgery. Radzinowicz cites an interesting passage in Lord Campbell's *Lives of the Chief Justices* (3rd ed., 1874) where

Campbell refers to "the then widespread belief that England's commercial credit required forgery to be punished by death" (in Radzinowicz's summary) and where Campbell, who lived from 1779 to 1861, goes on to add,

> I myself once heard a judge, at Stafford, thus conclude an address to a prisoner convicted of uttering a forged one-pound note, after having pointed out to him the enormity of the offence, and exhorted him to prepare for another world: "And I trust that, through the merits and mediation of our Blessed Redeemer, you may there experience that mercy *which a due regard to the credit of the paper currency of the country forbids you to hope for here.*"[41]

Doubtless we could all agree to label the first two examples given above as instances of verbal irony. But what should we do with this case? Most of us would surely experience some sense of irony upon reading this anecdote, but we might well locate this irony in ourselves rather than in the person of the hanging judge who actually spoke the words. In other words, we would not analyze this example as an instance of verbal irony on a par with the other two examples. A typical analysis might go something like this: Because of changes in values, in modes of expression, and even in the connotations of certain words, anyone reading the judge's statement today would find contradictions that make the statement absurd. We fasten on certain parts of the statement so that the judge seems to say that a person without sufficient "regard" for "paper" ought to be hanged. This judgment contradicts our basic, unspoken assumption that the punishment should fit the crime, and the contradiction seems to us so self-evident that the judge's statement is absurd on the face of it. Anyone making such a statement today could not possibly mean what he said and could only be speaking ironically. Thus, even though we recognize that in his own day the judge meant this statement exactly as he spoke it, nevertheless we feel irony in reading the judge's words because we cannot help reading anachronistically. We read as if the statement were spoken today.

This explanation tries to deal with the problem that a statement that seems self-evidently absurd to us must have seemed sensible to the person who spoke it, and to deal with this problem the explanation relies on a notion of the relativity of values and forms of expression. Other, analogous explanations would also be possible. But of course, if we had read the judge's statement in a piece of literature, we would not have had to explain away this difficulty. Suppose, for example, that the judge was a character in a novel, even in an eighteenth-century novel. We undoubtedly would have assumed that the contradiction we noted was so blatant that it could not have escaped the author of the novel and that, therefore, the author himself could not have shared the sentiments that he put in the mouth of his judge; on the contrary, the author must have used the judge's words to express ideas altogether opposed to what the judge says. For support in our instinctive reaction, we would surely recall that the unchristian inhumanity of English law is not an unfamiliar theme in eighteenth-century literature. But since the judge is a historical figure rather than a fictional character, there is no author standing behind him. So long as we assume that a person would not speak with such irony while he was sentencing a man to be hanged, we must conclude that the judge meant what he said, and there is no one—besides ourselves—to whom we can refer the "true" meaning that the judge's words require us to find behind them.

Or is there? It seems plausible to suppose that the irony that we so readily find in the judge's statement—and that surely certain eighteenth-century contemporaries of the judge, schooled just as he must have been in principles of Christianity and justice, would have found equally evident—does not arise merely in the eyes of the beholder. Rather (and this is really the only alternative), we can suppose that the irony was put there by the judge himself. But since the judge certainly was not aware that he was speaking ironically, we need to appeal to the Freudian idea of the unconscious to pursue this explanation. We must consider the possibility of unconscious irony. And if we can accept that such a phenomenon might exist, then we have an important connection between the conscious verbal irony we have examined in our first two examples and the irony often found in literature, in which a character innocently says one thing while the author means to say something quite different.

But what, in the present case, could motivate unconscious irony? Without knowing anything about the particular judge who pronounced these words, we can certainly speculate about a child who feels the oppressive weight of harsh parental strictures but whose open rebellion is too successfully repressed, either by the parents or by the child himself, to continue openly. In time, the child, through identification with the powerful parents, takes over their harsh rules into his own superego and no longer consciously feels them as belonging to an alien authority. Yet the secret rebellion continues, and the child's early evaluation of the laws of authority remains active in the adult's unconscious. The adult becomes a judge, perhaps precisely because of this hidden rebelliousness: the revolt against authority has seemed so dangerous and so threatening that the child has identified himself intensely with the punitive superego that, as a judge, he comes to personify. Yet in the very act of passing judgment on another person, the judge unconsciously sees himself as this other person, as the child who is being unfairly punished. And he murmurs against the very judgment that he is passing. He pronounces it in such a way that he brings out all of its harshness, its vengefulness, and its injustice. His attack is so muted that it remains unconscious to him, but nevertheless his words reveal an ironic mockery of the sentence he is meting out. The judge personifies and attacks a punitive authority at one and the same time.

Broadly speaking, all three examples we have analyzed are meant to open up the relevance of psychoanalytic psychology to the study of irony. At this preliminary stage, we need especially to emphasize the importance of the following principles of Freudian psychology. First, it is not possible for a person to say something that she does not (in some sense) mean. Therefore, we cannot view irony as a combination of something that the person does not mean and something that she does mean. All possible levels of an ironic statement have at least psychological meaning. Second, human beings develop a limitless variety of ways of expressing at one and the same time (or in rapid succession) contradictory wishes, impulses, desires, and meanings—at least one of which is usually unconscious. In fact, psychoanalysis rests almost entirely on Freud's understanding of the compromises entered into by such conflicting and contradictory wishes. Certainly irony would qualify as a compromise formation of this kind. For irony allows the ironist to express two or more conflicting ideas at once and to mean both or all of them. Rhetorical explanations of irony, in allowing the ironist "not to mean" what he says, in fact simply repeat a version of the ironist's own disingenuous defense, the defense of "I didn't really mean it." But a psychoanalytic approach would insist that the ironist did mean it and would look to see exactly what he meant.

In the first two examples we analyzed, the ironist was surely aware of saying contradictory things, but he was perhaps less aware of the extent to which he actually meant the thing that he seemed not to mean. In the third example, the irony undoubtedly never reached conscious awareness. In this case, the unconscious was the ironist—and such a subtle one that the conscious mind would never have heard the mockery. Literature imitates both of these forms of irony. As we have said, the first form it imitates in a straightforward fashion (as in the Austen example). The second form of irony literature imitates in a peculiar way, in that the conscious mind may be represented by a literary character while the ironizing unconscious is represented by the figure of the author who stands "behind" the literary character. Again, a character such as Lemuel Gulliver is an obvious example.

There are also transitional examples in literature, as, for instance, in Michael Drayton's sonnet "Since ther's no helpe, Come let us kisse and part":

> Since ther's no helpe, Come let us kisse and part,
> Nay, I have done: You get no more of Me,
> And I am glad, yea glad withall my heart,
> That thus so cleanly, I my Selfe can free,
> Shake hands for ever, Cancell all our Vowes,
> And when We meet at any time againe,
> Be it not seene in either of our Browes,
> That We one jot of former Love reteyne;
> Now at the last gaspe, of Loves latest Breath,
> When his Pulse fayling, Passion speechlesse lies,
> When Faith is kneeling by his bed of Death,
> And Innocence is closing up his Eyes,
>   Now if thou would'st, when all have given him over,
>   From Death to Life, thou might'st him yet recover.[42]

In this sonnet, there are clues from the very beginning that the speaker does not mean what he says when he tells the lady, "You get no more of me." As in most cases of irony, these clues result from apparent contradictions in what the speaker says—contradictions that often seem to result from exaggeration. Thus, when the speaker talks of "Cancell[ing] all our Vowes," he of course could not mean what he says if he is using the word "vows" in its strong, literal sense, that is, as something that cannot be canceled.

On the other hand, whereas marriage vows are actually vows, lovers' promises are not; so in order to make this statement self-contradictory, and therefore potentially ironic, the speaker has been engaging in exaggeration. But the point here is that, whereas the reader, from the very beginning, begins to pick up hints that the speaker is indulging in an ironic attack on his own dependence on the lady, the speaker himself only gradually articulates his awareness of this undercurrent in what he says. In other words, the speaker does not at first realize that he is speaking ironically and that he does not actually mean what he seems to be saying to the lady. In this example, then, the author is speaking ironically through the speaking voice, and yet because the speaker almost catches up to the author's irony, we cannot say that there are two distinct characters here. If anything, we could say that there is a certain time lag here—matching the real-life case in which a person only retrospectively realizes that her words contained certain ironic meanings.

THE PSYCHOANALYSTS ON IRONY

It remains for us, in this introduction, to review the significant efforts that have so far been made to analyze irony in terms of the insights of psychoanalysis.

The first important contribution was made by Theodor Reik, the Viennese nonmedical analyst and friend of Freud who received the letter analyzed above and who is mostly known today for the works he published in English after he emigrated to the United States. In 1932, however, Reik wrote an article on irony—"Grenzland des Witzes" [Borderland of the Joke]—that one would be tempted to call "pathbreaking," except that the path it cleared had few if any travelers and has long since been covered over by neglect.[43] Despite its fate, the article is extremely important for an understanding of irony, and I therefore summarize it in some detail.

As concerns irony, Reik's basic argument is that there is a connection to be made between ironic mockery and the latent mockery present in obsessive-compulsive symptoms. In his *Notes upon a Case of Obsessional Neurosis*, Freud himself had analyzed one of the Rat Man's obsessional ideas as self-punishment for unconscious irony directed at the patient's father and at "the lady whom he admired"; Reik, however, shows the ironic form of the obsessional ideas themselves.[44] Reik illustrates his point by giving the partial case history of a young nobleman whom Reik saw as a psychoanalytic patient and who suffered from obsessive thoughts. The patient, Reik says, showed particular respect for everything that was connected with noblemen or the nobility and a special contempt for servants. This was not simply the customary snobbery of a young man of the patient's class, since his respect for the nobility had about it something "obviously exaggerated, forced, and absurd" (300). Thus, for example, he called the Virgin Mary "countess" because he could not bear to think that a person so worthy of being honored should not have been of noble birth. On the other hand, he could barely think of waiters, servants, and soldiers as being human; a waiter he would think of as "the devil" and a serving girl as "the devil's wife." These thoughts, Reik tells us, surprised even the young man himself, an intelligent free-thinker who "on another psychic level" knew quite well that class differences did not determine human worth and who occasionally laughed at his own bizarre ideas. But what, Reik asks, does the patient *mean* by these obsessional thoughts (as the psychoanalyst labels them); what sense could they possibly have? To answer this question, Reik brings in the childhood history of the patient.

The patient came from an aristocratic East European family, and as a child he had become quite attached to several of the servants in the family household. His parents, however, who strongly believed in maintaining the proper social distances, tried to break the child of these attachments. In addition, the child had to witness numerous scenes in which the servants he was fond of were abused and mistreated. During this same period, the parents also began the child's instruction in religion and the Bible, often repeating to him the precepts about Christian humility and love of one's neighbor. When the child, precocious and observant, objected that Christians did not actually behave as he was being taught to, his remarks were branded as untrue and arrogant. In time, the boy's behavior toward the servants changed in accordance with his parents' wishes, and eventually he started having the fantasies already described.

In light of this early history, Reik interprets the patient's obsessive thoughts as an ironic conflation of the parents' teachings on the subjects of servants and Christianity. There was an obvious conflict between the parents' Christian precepts and their attitude toward the servants, but the boy was able to resolve it, in a way that did not contradict the opinions of his parents (which were very important to him), by making use of other religious teachings from the Bible, especially those about Satan. Reik continues:

> True Christians could act in such a humiliating and brutal manner only toward the devil—so ran the boy's ironic thought . . . In this way, not only had he consciously adopted his parents' views about the servants, but he had taken them to an extreme, indeed had heightened them to absurdity, for the purpose of a *reductio ad absurdum.* The unconscious meaning of these obsessive ideas is the most bitter mockery: "so that's how it is with the Christianity that you go on about all the time . . . A Christian could only treat the devil in this way—therefore these servants are not humans but devils." Consciously the obsessive idea has the meaning of being obedient to the parents' teachings; unconsciously it represents resentful mockery of these authorities. (301–2)

Reik then summarizes the similarities and differences he finds between the "pathological" phenomenon of obsessive ideas and the "normal" one of ironic expression. The most obvious difference is that the unconscious mockery in the obsessive idea remains hidden both from the obsessive himself and from those around him. This mockery has, moreover, only an "intrapsychic" function, whereas the mockery of irony can become socially useful.[45] As for similarities, Reik focuses on those of technique and purpose: "representation through the opposite, as well as exaggeration; the hidden character of the mockery, which for the most part uses allusion to reach its aim; the instinctually strong, aggressive purposes" (303). He adds the important refinement that representation through the opposite usually means representation through the *opponent*: "One unmasks the opponent by putting on the opponent's mask; one belittles him by putting oneself in his place" (303).

Reik explains the connection between irony and obsessive-compulsive symptoms by speculating (in a somewhat confusing manner) about a common infantile origin. In both, he says, we see "the mechanism of oral cannibalism," which "goes back to archaic [i.e., infantile] models of devouring and vomiting up the object that is both admired and hated" (304, "object" here is psychoanalytic jargon indicating an important other person.) The devouring is reflected in the "introjection" of the object, a process that depends on an unusually intense ambivalence toward the object. This ambivalence "makes possible the reversal of tender impulses into feelings of hatred, as we see them expressed in mockery. But it also makes possible the assimilation of the object's opinions, physical bearing, and mental attitudes, as this is reflected in irony" (304). To make Reik's argument more explicit, I would add that ambivalence comes out in the process of introjection, because introjection implies both a sadistic devouring of the object and also a process of identification by which the object is incorporated into the infant. In addition to this original ambivalence, reflected in the process of introjection/devouring, Reik seems to imply that there arises a second moment—a "disappointment in the object"—and a consequent depression. (Reik may, however, simply be equating this disappointment with one aspect of the original ambivalence.) As a mechanism for dealing with this depression, the infant "expels" the devalued object—after the model of vomiting—and this expulsion is reflected in ironic expression. Reik concludes (a bit inconsistently, given what he has just said) that "the embittered mockery which is concealed in irony and in the latent meaning of obsessive symptoms is only the distortion of an originally loving wish for identification" (304).

Finally, Reik explains that as a form of object devaluation, irony is a late development, since it makes almost exclusive use of representation through words and since in irony "words must stand for regressive actions" (304). Earlier, the object would have been represented physically, through gestures, movements, and mimicry—the accuracy of which would have been guaranteed by the underlying identification. And at that time irony could scarcely have been distinguished from caricature. Eventually, however, the physical signs, gestures, and mimicry become secondary to the ironic representation through words, and they then serve only as a kind of incidental hint to the listener that irony is present.

Reik later wrote again on irony, notably in *The Secret Self*, where he has a chapter ("Saint Irony") that develops one of the insights in his earlier work and applies it to the writings of Anatole France.[46] The direction Reik takes in this later essay strikes me as much less rigorously psychoanalytic than the article just summarized, and it is not a direction we will follow in the present investigation of irony. But the essay works out an interesting insight and may be valuable to some readers, especially for its analysis of France's story "Le Jongleur de Notre Dame" ("Our Lady's Juggler"). Hence I will quote briefly the theoretical proposition Reik tests here.

Reik starts with the perception that the audience of an ironic utterance has a momentary inclination to believe that the speaker meant what he said. Reik continues:

> The emotional process in the listener (or reader) must reflect directly or inadvertently something that took place during the production of the ironic sentence or representation. If there is a fleeting impulse to believe that the sentence heard is meant literally, there must have been at some time a similar impulse or inclination in the speaker himself. This inclination belongs perhaps to a past emotionally or intellectually long mastered. There was evidently a time at which the speaker of the ironic sentence approved of and respected the object or persons he deals with now in this form of concealed aggression . . . The creator of irony is for a moment tempted to lapse into an old faith, to give himself again to an overcome illusion . . . In the ironic expression not only are the old illusion and the old disenchantment reawakened from the past, but also the indignation and the bitterness, which are the more deeply felt, the more genuinely and sincerely the old faith was once embraced.[47]

Besides Reik, the other major psychoanalyst who has written on irony is Edmund Bergler, especially in his books *Laughter and the Sense of Humor* and *The Superego*.[48] Bergler's ideas on irony itself are quite reminiscent of Reik's, but he sets them in a somewhat different context by relating them to his overall theories of wit and humor, and ultimately to his theories of psychic masochism and the superego. Bergler's approach derives from his fundamental belief that "the unconscious ego sustains its very existence by producing its defensive weapons—wit, the comic, irony—in reply to the constant avalanche of reproaches emanating from unconscious conscience."[49] As this quotation suggests, Bergler for the most part lumps irony together with other forms of aggressive wit. He sees all such witticisms as having two basic purposes. First, though they may seem to be directed at external authorities, they are actually an attempt to debunk the internal images imprinted long ago by the authorities of the nursery; these images are found in the two parts of the unconscious superego— the ego ideal (the standards that we are trying to live up to) and what Bergler calls "Daimonion" (the enforcer that attacks the ego for not living up to the ideal). Thus, the ironic attack attempts to prove that the ideals are flawed (and therefore don't have to be lived up to) and that the enforcer is not as powerful as it seemed. Second, this "pseudo-aggression" against external authority is an attempt to "prove" that the individual is not passive and masochistic. We will develop Bergler's ideas about this second point more fully in chapters 2 and 3, but we should note here that, however eccentric this claim may seem, it is actually in line with mainstream psychoanalytic thought. For example, in his standard work *Basic Theory of Psychoanalysis*, Robert Waelder lists "fear of one's own masochism" as one of the basic forms of anxiety—so the need to deny this masochism would be widespread and paramount.[50]

As concerns irony specifically, Bergler makes two main points. First, he says that "*self-irony* is a preventive mechanism; it is designed to ward off an anticipated attack." He also takes note of its obvious masochistic elements.[51] Second, he takes up Reik's idea that neurotic symptoms may contain "a mocking irony directed against the internalized educators."[52] However, he explains this process not in terms of exaggeration but in terms of literal repetition:

> Moral precepts actually communicated to the child during the educational process, and later also embodied in the ego ideal, are secondarily reproduced literally by the unconscious ego, where literal repetition—at the *wrong* time, in the *wrong* place, on the *wrong* occasion, out of context and with *wrong* intention—does not reflect, but rather distorts, the meaning originally intended. The ironic technique of immobilizing Daimonion's power by speciously fulfilling the demands of the ego ideal (hence neutralizing the weapon of torture), corresponds to one of the few pseudo-aggressive retorts of the otherwise weak unconscious ego.[53]

This last sentence makes clear why Bergler wants to speak of exact repetition rather than exaggeration: through literal repetition, the ironist leaves her hands "absolutely clean" and can approach her conscience with a clear conscience. As an aside, we may add that this form of irony certainly exists even as conscious irony. For example, in a recent *New Yorker* cartoon by Ed Arno, a young boy is selling lemonade behind a "Lemonade—5¢" stand that he has set up on a sidewalk. Next to him, a middle-aged man is doing the same thing behind a slightly larger and more sophisticated booth. The caption has the man saying: "I started young, I liked it, and I just stayed with it"—an ironic send-up of every precept we have heard about stick-to-itiveness and career ambitions, with an exact literal repetition.[54]

Bergler, then, clearly sees the relationship between irony and hypocrisy, which he specifically takes up in his article "Hypocrisy: Its Implications in Neurosis and Criminal Psychopathology."[55] His point emerges clearly in the case study of a young man who was studying to become a pastor. The young man entered analysis with Bergler because his teachers in the protestant seminary, under the impression that he was a "hypocrite," were trying to dissuade him from his choice of profession. In analysis, the young man explained how he had decided, at the age of six, to become a minister. One Sunday the patient's father, a cruel and unjust disciplinarian, was giving the boy a beating for some unexplained offense but interrupted the punishment to take the family to church. During the service, the boy "was greatly impressed with the fact that his father, who a few minutes before was so autocratic and cruel, listened with devotion to the pastor" (613); at that moment he decided to become a minister, and he pursued this decision with even more satisfaction because his father strongly disapproved of it. Bergler, of course, had no doubt that the young man had chosen his profession for neurotic reasons and that his superiors were right to question the sincerity of his motives. But Bergler insists that this hypocrisy on the part of the young man was completely unconscious. In fact, the only way it manifested itself to the seminarian was in the obsessional thought—which began to torment him—that he would use blasphemous language in delivering his sermons. Indeed, the following incident actually did occur:

> All of the pupils of the seminary had to deliver "test" sermons in small churches. The young man did so and seemingly succeeded. However, he used such ambiguous language and quoted religious authorities in such a way that some protest came a few days after his test. A few of the members of the congregation wrote to the church, asking whether the quotations were correct. As it happened, they were, but the youth had used them in an objectionable manner, mentioning, for instance, the theological dispute during the arianic heresy as to whether God was

"homoousios" or "homoiousios" and elaborating at length over the small difference of an "i," "which was responsible for the death of many persons." Without knowing it consciously, the man was making fun of religion, neurotically projecting upon it his conflicts with his father and his defense mechanisms against him. (613–14)

We do not need to go further into Bergler's analysis of this case, but we should note that Bergler defines hypocrisy as "lip service instead of inner acceptance" (612). This definition would obviously cover verbal irony as well, except that, in irony, the lip service itself is contaminated by underlying beliefs that are in conflict with it. And indeed, Bergler's case clearly shows hypocrisy sliding over into irony. It is also of particular interest to us in the present study because of the obvious connections between the ironies in the young man's sermon and those that Swift levels, in *Gulliver's Travels*, against the brutal consequences of "insignificant" religious differences—Swiftian ironies that are, as we will see in the next chapter, actually quite difficult to account for.

Bergler's insights are further developed by W. N. Evans in his article "The Casuist: A Study in Unconscious Irony."[56] Bergler had emphasized the fact that when an authoritarian precept is repeated in inappropriate circumstances, the precept is effectively stated in an ironic mode, and the ironist is thereby debunking the precept. But Bergler had also noted that such inappropriate repetitions may also be used as a pseudo-moralistic excuse for neurotic behavior. Evans modifies and extends this latter idea by citing a number of examples of "simultaneously circumventing a taboo and literally obeying it" (406)—behavior that Evans connects with the dishonorable tradition of religious casuistry.

One patient, for example, was brought up in a puritanical household in which, as Evans says, "all the pleasures of the senses were condemned" (407). Included among the taboos was the drinking of alcoholic beverages, and the patient had even been forced to sign a pledge, at the age of five, renouncing all alcoholic drink. Evans cites, however, the following instance of casuistry in the patient's household:

Fanatically teetotal as the family were, they nevertheless brewed their own wines, which, by some act of moral juggling, were labeled "Temperance" and were to be drunk on social occasions only. In his dry manner the patient recalled that the conviviality

on these occasions was attributed to the spirit of good fellow-
ship rather than to the alcoholic content of the elderberry wine.
The logic was impeccable: as the wine was Temperance, it could
not, by definition, contain any alcohol. (407–8).

Use of the word *Temperance* here is an obvious instance of (unconscious) verbal irony and one that reveals particularly clearly the
double psychological purpose of irony. On the one hand, the irony
debunks the authoritarian precept, now absorbed into the superego strictures of the family members. But on the other, the ironists—the patient's family—receive total credit, so to speak, for
calling something by a name that is in fact the opposite of the true
name (the name that a conscious ironist would have intended as
his actual meaning). The ironists get credit for their words even
when they "don't mean them."

A second example—one that will have a ring of familiarity for
many ex-children—can serve to reinforce this point about irony.
An English patient of Evans remembered how her father, "a pre-
cisian in moral observances" (in Evans's phrase), had once set out
a bowl of prize strawberries, freshly picked, that he intended to
exhibit at a horticultural show. When he came back and found
that the top of each strawberry had been bitten off, he lined his six
children against a wall and questioned each of them; each denied
having committed the crime. Having, however, finally discovered
the guilty party—the patient, then eight years old—he angrily
charged her with having flagrantly lied to him as well. But the
patient stubbornly insisted on her innocence: "I said that I had not
eaten a single one. And that is true. I just bit the tops off" (402).

What, for our purposes, we want to notice here is not only the
little girl's casuistical interpretation of the injunction always to tell
the truth—an interpretation that might also be considered ironic
in that it allows her to call a lie the truth. But we also want to
notice how the little girl confidently relies on her ability to defend
herself by an appeal to the letter of her statement. As I tried to
show earlier in the chapter, a similar belief that defensive security
can be found in the literal level of an ironic utterance is one of the
principal features of irony—though the adult ironist (except perhaps insofar as she is dealing with the external constraints of legal
censorship) can no longer realistically defend this belief, and it
persists only as an unconscious determinant of verbal irony.

Besides the work of Reik, Bergler, and Evans, there are a few other scattered attempts to connect psychoanalysis and verbal irony. Notable among these are an article by H. Schneider, to be considered in chapter 3, and a recent Lacanian-Derridean analysis of irony by Vaheed K. Ramazani.[57] Ramazani emphasizes that "the essence of irony as a figure, the feature that distinguishes it from other figures, is its gesture of denial, repudiation, retraction, negation" (556). Yet rhetorical irony, with its apparent promise of a fixed, stable meaning that can be arrived at through translation, denies this denial: "We might say that it forcefully misspeaks, flagrantly misapprehends the condition of its own inscription, which is absence, alienation, castration" (553). This is a suggestive comment, and using a quite different kind of analysis, I have also tried above to show ways in which the ironist denies her denial; however, it is equally important to see how the ironist denies her *affirmation*, as we will discuss in subsequent chapters. Ramazani, of course, focuses on denial because he sees irony as paradigmatic of all language (given the Lacanian idea of language): "A negative unfolding, a repetition of the noncoincidence of word and world, self and other, irony reveals absence as the motor of all discourse and the determinant of all meaning. Indeed, every ironic signifier (and every signifier is, in this sense, ironic) designates conscious and unconscious signifieds with which it shares the common ground of difference, mutual exclusion" (555). In taking this step, however, by granting to irony this kind of paradigmatic status, Ramazani flattens out its specificity and sacrifices the particular psychological flavor that distinguishes irony from other kinds of discourse: it's like all other language, only more so. Ultimately, his analysis belongs more to the philosophy of language than to a psychodynamic theory of human behavior.

CHAPTER 2

Fantasy and Irony in Gulliver's Travels

The most striking, as well as the most obvious fact about Swift's *Gulliver's Travels* has never been sufficiently explicated, and that fact is the strange dual character of the book. On the one hand, *Gulliver's Travels* is an ironic satire against humans in general and against particular men and women whom Swift had observed in the England of his time. On the other hand, the book is a child's fantasy—especially its first two parts, the "Voyage to Lilliput" and the "Voyage to Brobdingnag." I do not mean simply that the book appeals to children, though the long-standing fascination that its first part has exerted over children certainly results from the genuineness of its child's fantasy. Rather, the very plot—and therefore the "soul" of the book—reenacts, in a way that we will explore here, typical infantile fantasies that according to psycho-analysis never die out but persist in the adult unconscious. It is these fantasies that actually determine the structure of Swift's book, and from the point of view of plot it is the irony that attaches itself opportunistically to the fantasy.[1]

But how exactly should we connect the irony and the fantasy? Clearly the traditional humanistic and rhetorical view of irony will not help. Many readers have subscribed to Swift's official view that he was aiming to correct the morals and manners of humankind, and these readers would naturally consider the irony as one of the rhetorical devices at Swift's disposal in accomplish-ing this end.[2] To such readers, the child's plot must be irrelevant at best and more likely an embarrassment. An embarrassment, that is, because these readers have often felt compelled to defend Swift against that large camp who, from Swift's time on, have been repulsed by the scatology and the misanthropy of *Gulliver's Travels*. Those who would rehabilitate Swift as a humanist work-ing for the betterment of the human race have had to look away from—or explain away—the very aspects of the book that most unfailingly would delight a child.[3]

If, however, we are willing to look from a psychoanalytic point of view at the psychological basis of irony, then we should certainly expect to find an intimate connection between the irony of a book like *Gulliver's Travels* and the semidisguised infantile fantasies that make up its plot. Both, of course, could be traced back to the psychobiography of the author, Jonathan Swift.[4] But we do not need to take this final step into biography in order to investigate the connections between the irony and the fantasy that we find in the book. The fantasy itself should provide us with most of the evidence we need for understanding the psychology at work in the novel.

A writer may be moved for his own neurotic reasons, and under special psychological conditions, to elaborate in an imaginative fiction the infantile fantasies that he cannot otherwise lay to rest. But the fantasies themselves will tend to be common ones: the variations within infantile fantasies, and their ultimate vicissitudes in adulthood, may show a certain range of difference, but psychoanalysis has succeeded in finding a certain number of basic patterns that are shared by large numbers of people in our culture. Thus, for example, we may assimilate the fantasies that lie behind *Gulliver's Travels* to a certain *type* of infantile fantasy without necessarily connecting them to the hypothetical specificity of Swift's own psychobiography. It is, indeed, this typicality that we are after. For if verbal irony is a fairly common brand of human behavior, then its psychological determinants are likely to show certain similarities in many who resort to this behavior. And naturally one way to analyze these psychological determinants is to examine the fantasies that tend to appear along with the irony. A work like *Gulliver's Travels* gives us an obvious opportunity for doing precisely this—especially since it is, as the psychoanalyst I. F. Grant Duff has said of all Swift's work, "full of an amazing wealth of the sort of fantasy which is usually unconscious."[5] Moreover, as I will show in chapters 3 and 4, when we look at a very different work like Franz Kafka's *The Trial*, fantasies emerge that are remarkably similar and that, although they are somewhat less overt than those in *Gulliver's Travels*, assume an equally dominant position in the structure of the novel. This similarity will help us to confirm our conclusions about the psychological profile of irony when considered from a psychoanalytic point of view.

THE "VOYAGE TO LILLIPUT"

The most powerful fantasy contained in *Gulliver's Travels*, and the one of most interest to us for its connection to irony, lies behind the story of part 1, "A Voyage to Lilliput." This fantasy mixes elements from two different stages of the child's development. In the basic situation—the données of part 1—the fantasy shows connections to the earliest stages of infantile megalomania. The actual plot, however, develops as an oedipal drama, specifically as a fantasy of crime, punishment, and evasion. Indeed, it may well be that all *plots*—the actions imitated in literature— derive from the oedipal situation but that the motives, the fears, and the desires that activate the work and determine its character always go further back, to preoedipal stages. This double origin, affecting as it does both the plot and something less easily definable, which perhaps we can only call the "shape" or the "contour" of a work, is readily visible in the "Voyage to Lilliput," and we will look at each of the two elements in turn.

It is obvious enough that the Gulliver of part 1 is, in many ways, in the position of an infant. When he first wakes up after the shipwreck, he is as immobilized and helpless as if he were in swaddling clothes. The Lilliputians bring him food and drink, and later on, after they have put him in his crib of a cathedral, they also begin to clothe him and carry away his excrement.

Psychologically, Gulliver also exhibits one of the main characteristics that psychoanalysis teaches us to expect in the very young child—infantile megalomania. Gulliver believes himself to be a powerful giant compared to these undersized Lilliputians who feed and clothe him and take care of his bodily excretions. He is the center of their world, the focus of all their concerns, and thousands of them cater to him just so that he can have a single good meal. Six hundred persons are attached to him as "Domesticks," but in fact the entire state enters into his service, even the Emperor, who "gave Assignments upon his Treasury" to take care of Gulliver.[6]

Of course, Swift presents Gulliver's infantile, megalomaniacal fantasy as a reality: in the terms of the book, Gulliver really *is* a giant being served by these diminutive providers. But we notice a curious fact about Gulliver's own belief in this "reality": he never acts in accordance with his belief. When Gulliver wakes up to find himself tied down and surrounded by the Lilliputians, he struggles to get loose until they attack him with volleys of arrows; then he ceases to struggle:

> I thought it the most prudent Method to lie still; and my Design was to continue so till Night, when my left Hand being already loose, I could easily free myself: And as for the Inhabitants, I had Reason to believe I might be a Match for the greatest Armies they could bring against me, if they were all of the same Size with him that I saw. (1.1.6)

Shortly after this moment, the Lilliputians begin dancing on Gulliver's breast, provoking these sentiments in Gulliver:

> I confess I was often tempted, while they were passing backwards and forwards on my Body, to seize Forty or Fifty of the first that came in my Reach, and dash them against the Ground. But the Remembrance of what I had felt, which probably might not be the worst they could do; and the Promise of Honour I made them, for so I interpreted my submissive Behaviour, soon drove out those Imaginations. Besides, I now considered my self as bound by the Laws of Hospitality to a People who had treated me with so much Expence and Magnificence. However, in my Thoughts I could not sufficiently wonder at the Intrepidity of these diminutive Mortals, who durst venture to mount and walk on my Body, while one of my Hands was at Liberty, without trembling at the very Sight of so prodigious a Creature as I must appear to them. (1.1.8)

In both of these passages, Gulliver insists on his superior strength, on his ability to overcome the Lilliputians; however, in each case he refuses to test his strength against them. In explaining this refusal, Gulliver refers to "adult" virtues. First he talks about "prudence," which teaches him to choose a better time to counterattack. Of course, the better time never arrives; "Fortune," as Gulliver says, "disposed otherwise of me" (1.1.6). In the second passage, Gulliver moves to an even higher—more adult, more rational, more moral—plane of rationalization. Now he is talking about honor and promises and being bound by laws of hospitality. But we have no trouble seeing that Gulliver's self-restraint, which he portrays as something noble and as a triumph over a temptation that he now claims to "confess," has little to do with the lofty ideals he adduces. We notice how quickly Gulliver moves from "the Remembrance of what I had felt" (i.e., from his fear of further punishment) to the spurious "Promise of Honour," which no one could seriously accuse Gulliver of having made by virtue of his previous "submissive Behaviour."

Gulliver is defending himself here, but not against the charge that he seems to be refuting. He accuses himself of wanting to behave aggressively and defends himself by saying that he nonetheless acted morally, suppressing his aggressive urge. But as Edmund Bergler emphasizes throughout his psychoanalytic work, the real crime here is not aggression but masochism. Gulliver allows the Lilliputians to tie him down, "walk all over him," and sting him painfully with their volleys of arrows. But still he doesn't react. Why not?

Let us suppose for a moment that Gulliver is a child among the adult Lilliputians. As a child he receives a great deal of attention and care from the adults, and this treatment only serves to confirm his infantile megalomania, the idea that he is the center of the world and that the people around him exist only to fulfill his needs. On the other hand, his megalomania is offended by other kinds of treatment—by punishments and restrictions—as well as by some dawning sense of reality, by a sense that the adults are truly more powerful than he is and by a sense that he actually needs them if his wishes are to be satisfied. But Gulliver's megalomania rescues itself from these dangerous facts, and it does so in two ways.

In the first place, he simply denies, and indeed reverses, the facts. He, the child, becomes the giant, while the adult providers turn into midgets. On the other hand, he unconsciously knows better than to test this megalomaniacal fantasy because the fantasy would not survive the test of reality. The child could not win in a contest of strength against the powerful adults. It is this untested fantasy that lies behind part 1 of *Gulliver's Travels*. To be sure, the fantasy is presented as a reality, but the literary reality contains clues that show its origins in infantile megalomaniacal fantasy. Gulliver somehow knows that he cannot test his strength against the Lilliputians, but he protects himself against this knowledge by inventing excuses that show him, not as weak and fearful, but as a rational, moral adult. But this child's idea of adult morality is skewed: he sees promises of honor where none actually exist.

In this first method of rescuing the infant's megalomania— denial of the true power relations—we see that a corresponding sense of reality remains imbedded in the fantasy. Therefore, the fantasy is in some ways an inadequate solution to the problem of how to preserve infantile megalomania in the face of the infant's real situation. A second, more devious and ultimately more troublesome, solution is for the infant to believe that she herself wills whatever happens to her, even if those experiences are unpleasant or even punitive. If the powerful adults restrict or discipline her, they do so because the infant desires them to. This solution has been described by Bergler, and, as he points out, it traps the infant into masochistic wishes and behavior. Later the child may unconsciously provoke the parents into punishing her, thereby confirming in a masochistic way the power she has over them.[7]

Such masochistic behavior certainly characterizes Gulliver at many points. Gulliver reports, for example, that in the time after his arrival, as he subsequently learned,

> the Court was under many Difficulties concerning me. They apprehended my breaking loose; that my Diet would be very expensive, and might cause a Famine. Sometimes they determined to starve me, or at least to shoot me in the Face and Hands with poisoned Arrows, which would soon dispatch me: But again they considered, that the Stench of so large a Carcase might produce a Plague in the Metropolis, and probably spread through the whole Kingdom. (1.2.16)

What strikes one about this passage is, on the one hand, Gulliver's lack of any emotional response to the unjust punishments the court was considering, and, on the other, his very identification with the court in its deliberations over his fate. In other words, Gulliver gets to consider himself as one of the powerful adults, but he pays a heavy price for doing so: he must be willing to consider "objectively" and from the adults' point of view the punishments to be inflicted on him. He makes some attempt to reassert his fantasized superiority by referring to his giant body—but this giant body has been slaughtered and is now a "Carcase."In this passage, we can scarcely escape the sense of pleasure, only some of which derives from Gulliver's "triumph" over the adults who want to punish him but who would incur danger by doing so; much of the pleasure seems tinged with masochism.

As further evidence of Gulliver's masochism we might simply mention the famous incident in which Gulliver extinguishes the fire in the Queen's apartment by urinating on the palace. Gulliver reports that after performing this task,

> I returned to my House, without waiting to congratulate with
> the Emperor; because, although I had done a very eminent Piece
> of Service, yet I could not tell how his Majesty might resent the
> Manner by which I had performed it: For, by the fundamental
> Laws of the Realm, it is Capital in any Person, of what Quality
> soever, to make water within the Precincts of the Palace. (1.5.40)

In other words, Gulliver knew all along what punishment he was
likely to receive. Yet he need not consider that he acted in such a
way as to be punished, for he has turned his action into a "service" and therefore—or so he may tell himself—he neither willed
nor expected the punishment. Our neurotic rationalizations are
strongest when reality itself seems to make them irrefutable, as in
the present case. Certainly no outsider would argue with Gulliver
that he did the right thing in choosing the lesser of two evils, in
saving the Queen's apartment even if he has to violate the law. But
a rationalization is still a rationalization, even if it receives support from the realities of the situation. Gulliver's uneasiness shows
that he did not really expect the Lilliputians to deal fairly with his
moral dilemma. He provokes the Emperor into punishing him.

So we find that Gulliver does indeed make use of this second
defense against encroachments on his infantile megalomania—the
defense, that is, of masochism. But this defense, like the halluci-
nated power-reversal, is flawed. To the extent that a person unconsciously knows that he is behaving masochistically, that he is either
passively cooperating with his more powerful punishers or indeed
even provoking them into retaliating against him, then to this
extent his megalomaniacal fantasies have been strongly undermined. The masochism, therefore, must itself be unequivocally
denied. Indeed, so must anything that smacks of passive suffer-
ance, of a refusal to exercise the superior powers that the infant—
and later, unconsciously, the adult—believes himself to possess.

The denial of masochism, and of passivity generally, figures
throughout the "Voyage to Lilliput." Gulliver's feistiness, his spoil-
ing for a fight, and his sporadic bursts of activity all work to cover
up his basic servility and the masochism of his defensive maneuvers
against this servility. As Bergler observes, a person will often use a
show of aggression as a way of denying passivity; Bergler proposes,
as a test of whether aggression is actually "pseudo-aggression"—
that is, used strictly as an intrapsychic defense against self-accusa-
tions of masochism—that one see if the aggression is purposeful

either in defending the person or in getting what that person wants.[8] By such a test, Gulliver's aggressiveness looks weak.

We may gain some perspective on Gulliver's masochism in part 1, and the denial of this masochism, by looking at Gulliver's behavior in part 2, the "Voyage to Brobdingnag." The reversal in size relations shows us that something odd has happened to the basic fantasy of the "Voyage to Lilliput." The relative sizes of Gulliver and his hosts now reflect the true power relations existing between the infant (Gulliver) and the adults who take care of him. Indeed, the power relations have become fantastically exaggerated, for there is no possibility that Gulliver might ever attain the size and status of these powerful adults. Gulliver is stuck in an infantile position, and he knows it and likes it.

Part 2 represents, in fact, Gulliver's surrender to infantile passive wishes: as in Lilliput, all of his needs are taken care of, but the obfuscations with which, in Lilliput, he disguises his fundamental dependency have almost vanished. He is no longer being served by his inferiors but by his betters. To be sure, Gulliver's psyche works against this perception through the process of identification; that is, Gulliver fixes his attention—and probably his envy—so rigidly on the superior Brobdingnagians that he cannot bear to conceive himself as not being the same as they. So he tries to forget that he is different: in Brobdingnag, as Gulliver relates, "I could never endure to look in a Glass after mine Eyes had been accustomed to such prodigious Objects; because the Comparison gave me so despicable a Conceit of my self" (2.8.131), and even upon Gulliver's return to England he still imagines himself to be of Brobdingnagian stature: "My Wife ran out to embrace me, but I stooped lower than her Knees, thinking she could otherwise never be able to reach my Mouth" (2.8.133). But within *Gulliver's Travels*, this fantasy is presented as a fantasy—and one subject to being undermined at any moment by a chance look in a mirror or by any of the humiliating incidents that constantly remind Gulliver of his true place in the Brobdingnagian great chain of being. So Gulliver's fantasies of identification are not really very effective in disguising Gulliver's situation even from himself. Certainly, they have nothing like the power of the megalomaniacal fantasies of part 1, which seem to have created the very reality presented by the book—though in the imperfect way precisely described by Borges when he speculates about the reality of the *real* world:

"The greatest magician (Novalis has memorably written) would be the one who would cast over himself a spell so complete that he would take his own phantasmagorias as autonomous appearances. Would not this be our case?" I conjecture that this is so. We (the undivided divinity operating within us) have dreamt the world. We have dreamt it as firm, mysterious, visible, ubiquitous in space and durable in time; but in its architecture we have allowed tenuous and external crevices of unreason which tell us it is false.[9]

Part 2, of course, also has its phantasmagoria—the hallucination that Gulliver will never be as large as the powerful adults—and its "crevices of unreason"—the *avis ex machina* who carries Gulliver, willingly or unwillingly, out of this never-never land where he does not have to grow up. But the phantasmagoria is now, so to speak, on the other side. No longer does it support wishes for power and autonomy—even, as we will see, oedipal wishes to defeat and to displace the father. Rather, it supports the contrary wishes for surrender and passivity. In the land of Lilliput, Gulliver assumes a high social role and performs vital, adult acts; in Brobdingnag, his only function is to please and to amuse, to act the part of a puppet on a string. Fantasies of identification hardly counteract the passive wishes that dominate in the second voyage.

So part 2 looks very much like a regression in the psychoanalytic sense of the term, or even in a simple developmental sense. As in any regression, infantile tendencies that have been more or less covered over return once again to prominence, so that the passive and masochistic wishes that in part 1 are defended against, and to some extent concealed, now reemerge full blown. The passive tendencies are obvious enough, since Gulliver allows his needs to be taken care of by others—as he did in part 1, though again the tone is different in part 2, since Gulliver's main provider is a young girl who labels herself his "Nurse." As for the masochistic tendencies, we should consider how much more Gulliver appears as a passive victim in Brobdingnag than he did in Lilliput—by comparing, for example, the way in which Gulliver leaves Lilliput and then Blefuscu to the way in which he is carried off from Brobdingnag. Then, too, throughout his sojourn in Brobdingnag Gulliver subtly provokes and participates in his own degradation and humiliation. He describes, for example, a walk he took with Glumdalclitch:

> There was a Cow-dung in the Path, and I must needs try my
> Activity by attempting to leap over it. I took a Run, but unfortu-
> nately jumped short, and found my self just in the Middle up to
> my Knees . . . [T]he Queen was soon informed of what had
> passed, and the Footmen spread it about the Court; so that all
> the Mirth, for some Days, was at my Expence. (2.5.108)

One might object that we are witnessing in this example, not Gulliver's masochism, but rather Swift's sadism in putting his protagonist through a series of petty humiliations. Indeed, a focus on Swift
himself would obviously be relevant here. For we are surely dealing
with yet another instance in which literature allows an author to
split up his own psychic tendencies and deploy them in such a way
that they are represented as separate entities—so that, in the present case, Swift gets to gratify sadistic wishes, by inflicting pain on
the character he has created, while at the same time he indulges
masochistic wishes because he is himself not really separate from
this character who speaks with Swift's own "I." (In ordinary situa-
tions outside of literature, such splitting can be accomplished
through less obvious means of identification: for example, the
sadist who, as he inflicts punishment, simultaneously identifies
with the person receiving the punishment.) Nonetheless, we may
be able to make some distinction between an author's sadism (or
sadomasochism) and a character's masochism. In Gogol's "Overcoat," for example, the author's sadism seems to predominate. "A
creature had vanished and departed whose cause no one had cham-
pioned, who was dear to no one, of interest to no one," Gogol the
narrator writes of his hero Akaky Akakievich, "who never
attracted the attention of a naturalist, though the latter does not
disdain to fix a common fly upon a pin and look at him under the
microscope."[10] But, of course, this is precisely the kind of attention
Gogol pays to his protagonist, and the image is apt, in that Gogol is
like the scientist experimenting with a noxious insect and then
observing the results of the experiment; the sadistic impulses lying
behind this process seem obvious. But even in part 2 of *Gulliver's
Travels*, where Gulliver is most like a noxious insect, the distance
between Gulliver and his creator never yawns as wide as in "The
Overcoat"—probably for two reasons: first, the use of an "I"-nar-
rator and, second, the feeling Swift conveys that Gulliver is adapting realistically to a fantastic situation, adapting in fact in the same
way that any of us might do. As a result, we are struck not so much

by the sadism of a distant author as by the hidden pleasure Gulliver takes in his masochistic abasement.

It is precisely this pleasure in giving in to passive and masochistic wishes that psychoanalytic theory finds so dangerous to the development of the ego. The danger, moreover, is understood not just by the psychoanalytically trained observer, but even by the individual herself. At a very primitive level, passive and masochistic wishes interfere with the individual's ability to separate from the mother, and throughout life these wishes will represent to the individual a regression to the infantile period before separation and individuation. The difficulty with these wishes is in fact twofold: first, they obviously interfere with the ego's efforts to achieve active mastery, but second, because of what they represent to the ego, the ego tries to repress, or at least contain, these wishes. One way it does so it to make these wishes deeply shameful; another way, as Bergler explains, is to deny their existence by acting so aggressively that the ego misses the proof of its own passive-masochistic wishes. As elsewhere in psychoanalytic theory, the need to repress dangerous and unacceptable wishes takes its own toll, quite apart from the realistic danger of the wishes themselves. Indeed, in Bergler's (extreme) view, all neurosis results from the attempt to defend against one's masochistic wishes.

We have seen that in the "Voyage to Lilliput" Gulliver denies his masochistic wishes in a fairly successful manner. But what, then, happens in part 2, where even the basic fantasy represents a pleasurable surrender to passive and masochistic wishes? Obviously, Swift has to distance himself as much as possible from the content of his fantasy by making Gulliver, his representative in this fantasy, thoroughly foolish and reprehensible. But in addition, as I have indicated above, Gulliver himself is realistically portrayed as having to hide from his own feelings of worthlessness—feelings that are naturally generated by the pleasure he takes in his passive and masochistic existence. He cannot look in a mirror. He can only imagine himself, through identification, to be one of the giant Brobdingnagians.

In psychoanalytic theory, identification normally contributes to development, but here it seems to be a step backwards, a regression. This impression is confirmed if we consider how Gulliver's tendency to identify develops in the fourth part, the "Voyage to the Country of the Houyhnhnms." We see, in fact, that Gulliver's psychological stability deteriorates in the plot sketched out by parts 1, 2, and 4 and that this deterioration is reflected in the identifications that Gulliver enters into.[11] (Part 3, the "Voyage to Laputa," was written after the other three books and does not enter easily into the plot that culminates naturally in the voyage to the Houyhnhnms.) In the last part, the feelings of shame and worthlessness that Gulliver conceals in Brobdingnag become too intolerable to be contained, and we see Gulliver resorting to a psychic mechanism sometimes known as "projective identification." In simple *projection*, the individual imagines that certain (usually unacceptable) feelings or impulses belong not to the individual herself, but to someone in the outside world. In *projective identification*, the individual actually identifies with the person on whom she has projected these impulses. Clearly Gulliver's relation to the Yahoos can be characterized as one of projective identification, even though the underlying fantasy is, again, presented as real in the terms of the book. For the Yahoos represent those aspects of human sexuality and aggressiveness that most terrify Gulliver, and doubtless Swift as well. Moreover, Gulliver's shameful secret in part 4 is that he identifies himself precisely as one of these Yahoos. In the face of this devastating underlying identification, Gulliver has little choice but to attempt a more consciously pursued identification with the good authority figures, the Houyhnhnms. Gulliver is more desperate now than he was in Brobdingnag; the ever-deepening regression that characterizes Gulliver's movement through the book is confirmed by the fact that he has no longer been able to contain his own feelings of shame and worthlessness but has had to project them outward, even as he identifies with them in their new form. Therefore, his counteridentification with the Houyhnhnms is much more crucial to him now than was his identification with the Brobdingnagians. It is also, of course, no more effective than his earlier one, and yet Swift makes wonderfully clear the ludicrous extent to which Gulliver attempts to maintain his identification with the horses.

It is not altogether evident why Gulliver's regression should deepen as the book goes along, but we may speculate that the downward spiral is set off by the oedipal struggle that Gulliver wages in part 1. The struggle, in fact, takes on an almost classic outline, and we will look now at how this oedipal conflict develops between Gulliver and the emperor and at how it is influenced by the basic megalomaniacal fantasy that, we have said, underlies the "Voyage to Lilliput."[12]

Here is how Gulliver describes the emperor on first seeing him:

> He is taller by almost the Breadth of my Nail, than any of his Court; which alone is enough to strike an Awe into the Beholders . . . He was then past his Prime, being twenty-eight Years and three Quarters old, of which he had reigned about seven, in great Felicity, and generally victorious . . . He held his Sword drawn in his Hand, to defend himself, if I should happen to break loose; it was almost three Inches long, the Hilt and Scabbard were Gold enriched with Diamonds. (1.2.14–15)

About this passage, let us note first of all the simple fact that it is full of irony. Although we think of *Gulliver's Travels* as an ironic book, the irony in fact comes and goes, and this passage gives us a typical example of where it actually shows up: when needed to undermine power and authority. The actual technique used in the irony here is also important. Gulliver, the "neutral" observer, repeats almost in the form of free indirect style the feelings and opinions of others; but Gulliver obscures the fact that these judgments belong to others (that he is speaking in a kind of free indirect style) and presents them as if they were so generally accepted that, naturally, he too endorses them. However, Gulliver also presents the facts on which these judgments and feelings are based, and unfortunately *res ipsa loquitur*; no normal, right-thinking (non-Lilliputian) person would draw from these facts the conclusions that Gulliver mouths. Thus, if we analyzed Gulliver as a real person, by virtue of his citing these facts we would suspect either conscious or unconscious irony; that is to say, we would assume that he was saying something both positively and negatively at the same time and that this double, contradictory message was intended for his audience. But we sometimes tend not to analyze Gulliver as a real person. Gulliver—we are tempted to think—is a relatively "flat" character, a persona, a convenience; and such a character would not be entitled to an unconscious. So when, as in the present case, Gulliver is obviously not speaking with any *conscious* irony, we attribute the irony to Swift, thereby making the split between the author and his "I"-figure more absolute than it is. As I will try to show, we can match the richness of *Gulliver's Travels* only if we are aware of the psychic dramas being played out in the figure of Gulliver, and for these to make sense we must attach an unconscious to this "flat" character.[13]

One final note on the ironic technique in this passage. We normally think of irony as a simultaneous phenomenon, and in fact Paul de Man's most useful insight in his famous article on irony, "The Rhetoric of Temporality," was that irony could be seen as collapsed narrative, insofar as narrative moves between two moments whose structures are mutually contradictory.[14] Technically, the ironic aspects of the quoted passage all show this quality of simultaneity. The word *Sword,* for example, has the simultaneous double meaning of "sword" and "You call that puny thing a sword? That's no sword!" But we notice that this second meaning is added only retroactively, when Gulliver goes on to mention that "it was almost three Inches long"—so that here, and elsewhere in the passage, the true doubleness of a phrase comes across only after a momentary delay. The irony here begins to show a certain rhythm not unlike that in the actions of an obsessive-compulsive—for example, the man who, before getting into bed, carefully arranges his shoes so that they point out at a right angle from the bed, then gets out of bed again to arrange them parallel to the bed, and then back and forth again and again until he drops off to sleep from exhaustion.

In the actual content of the excerpted passage we have no trouble discerning the ambivalence generated by conflicts of the oedipal period. On the one hand, Gulliver stands in awe of the emperor, his height, his victorious reign, and his magnificent sword. These feelings correspond, of course, to the "negative" oedipal desires of the male child, whereby the child wishes to be the passive sexual object of the powerful father. On the other hand, the ironic undercurrent of the quoted sentences betrays the fearful competitiveness of the "positive" oedipal wishes, according to which the male child wishes to replace the father and win the sexual love of the mother. Thus, when Gulliver talks about the emperor's size, he manages to insinuate that a significant proportion of the emperor's height is, to Gulliver, no more than the breadth of his nail. He also accuses the emperor of being "past his Prime," at twenty-eight; here again, the fantasy of part 1 validates Gulliver's wishful judgment that a twenty-eight-year-old father is no longer a worthy adversary, and at the same time it allows him to feel he is being factual rather than covetous and competitive, since Lilliputians age at a different rate than Englishmen. Finally, while seeming to praise the emperor's sword—that is, penis—he also lets us know in the same breath that it is "almost three Inches long."

Gulliver's ambivalence about exposing and comparing his sword-penis to the emperor's may, indeed, stand for the contradictory oedipal mixture of fear, awe, contempt, and competitiveness that he generally exhibits toward the emperor. When emissaries of His Majesty come to search Gulliver—"for probably I might carry about me several Weapons, which must needs be dangerous Things, if they answered the Bulk of so prodigious a Person"—Gulliver replies that "his Majesty should be satisfied, for I was ready to strip my self, and turn up my Pockets before him" (1.2.17). Gulliver, that is, is willing to assume a passive female posture before the emperor and to allow the emperor to inspect his "Pockets." But while Gulliver seems sincere in making this declaration, he does not in fact quite live up to its letter, for he conceals a "secret Pocket which I had no Mind should be searched, wherein I had some little Necessaries of no Consequence to any but my self" (1.2.18). If we think of Gulliver as the child who has oedipal designs on the mother, then he is not quite being ingenuous in claiming that this private possession does not concern the emperor. Here, as elsewhere, we see evidence of Gulliver's bad faith.

Immediately afterwards, Gulliver's scimitar takes on the symbolic value of this private possession. Gulliver, whose eyes are "wholly fixed upon his Majesty," is ordered by the latter

> to draw my Scymiter, which, although it had got some Rust by the Sea-Water, was in most Parts exceeding bright. I did so, and immediately all the Troops gave a Shout between Terror and Surprize; for the Sun shone clear, and the Reflexion dazzled their Eyes, as I waved the Scymiter to and fro in my Hand. His Majesty, who is a most magnanimous Prince, was less daunted than I could expect; he ordered me to return it into the Scabbard, and cast it on the Ground as gently as I could, about six Foot from the End of my Chain. (1.2.20)

Gulliver, operating within the "realities" of the basic fantasy, "knows" that his sword is much larger and more dangerous than the emperor's, and he is therefore willing to expose it to the emperor, hoping to dazzle this monarch who so far has seemed rather to dazzle Gulliver. The emperor, however, is operating under a different reality—which perhaps we could call "adult reality" (the adult male knows that his penis is larger than the child's)—and refuses to be impressed with Gulliver's sword; in fact, he forces

Gulliver to surrender it. In matching swords with the emperor, Gulliver suffers a symbolic castration, and it is no surprise that a few lines later he tries to cover over this symbolic defeat by reiterating that "one private Pocket" has still "escaped their Search"; in it he has several "little Conveniences; which being of no Consequence to the Emperor, I did not think myself bound in Honour to discover; and I apprehended they might be lost or spoiled if I ventured them out of my Possession" (1.2.21). He knows better now than to try to overawe the emperor with his possessions, but he still tries to achieve a substitute effect by impressing the emperor's guards. Thus, when His Majesty's troops march under Gulliver, who is standing astride "like a *Colossus*," Gulliver is happy "to confess the Truth" that "my Breeches were at that Time in so ill a Condition, that they afforded some Opportunities for Laughter and Admiration" (1.3.26).

In Freud's description of the Oedipus complex, the cause of the boy's rivalry with his father and the focus of his oedipal strivings are his desire to possess the mother. In the "Voyage to Lilliput," the mother is represented by Her Imperial Majesty, the emperor's wife; and although she seems a marginal character, Gulliver's indirect encounter with her in the famous episode when he extinguishes the palace fire forms the central incident in part 1. The empress's marginality is, indeed, a good example of Freudian displacement, and the episode in question represents Gulliver's desperate confrontation with the oedipal parents, in which he tries to replace the father and win over the mother. And although he fantasizes victory—just as he did when he exposed his sword to the emperor—he actually experiences a crushing oedipal defeat that begins the spiralling regression from which he suffers throughout the remainder of the book.

The incident began, Gulliver tells us, when "several of the emperor's Court making their Way through the Croud, intreated me to come immediately to the Palace, where her Imperial Majesty's Apartment was on fire, by the Carelessness of a Maid of Honour, who fell asleep while she was reading a Romance. I got up in an Instant" (1.5.39). The maid of honor is an obvious displacement/stand-in for the empress-mother, so that the romantic flames consuming the empress's apartment represent either the mother's sexual desires or even—and this is most probable here—the parents' act of intercourse that has awakened the child Gulliver. The emperor-father's ostensible absence from this scene of the mother's uncontrolled sexual passion merely represents one of the conditions the child must fantasize in order to smooth the way for the fantasied triumph over the father: the child gets to possess the mother without actually having to imagine that he is pushing the father aside and replacing him as the mother's sexual partner. Thus, when Gulliver urinates on the empress's apartments, he accomplishes two things in terms of the oedipal fantasy underlying this scene. When he is awakened by his parents, envy and jealousy demand first of all that he put a stop to their intercourse; this he does, symbolically, by quenching the fire that is consuming the empress's rooms (Freud thought that in dreams a room often stands for female genitals). Gulliver's method is especially appropriate in that his urine pollutes the apartments, rendering them unfit for the uses to which they have been put—we learn that the empress subsequently moved to the other side of the palace, "firmly resolved that those Buildings should never be repaired for her Use" (1.5.40). But the second aim Gulliver accomplishes in this fantasy is actually to have intercourse with the mother himself. The intercouse enacted here is a child's skewed understanding of the sexual act (preserved in an adult, this understanding would be labelled perverse), according to which the male contribution is urine, "which I voided in such a Quantity,"—says Gulliver—"and applied so well to the proper Places, that in three Minutes the Fire was wholly extinguished" (1.5.40). So in this aspect of the fantasy, Gulliver is able to satisfy the mother through his prodigious "sexual" feat.

When we associate these psychological undercurrents with Gulliver, a curious thing begins to happen: some of Gulliver's statements look very ironic indeed, and the irony seems to belong, not to an author behind the screen, but to this character's own unconscious. Thus, at the precise moment we have been discussing, when Gulliver has extinguished the fire, Gulliver can fantasize unconsciously that he has won an oedipal victory over the emperor-father. But the child does not get to indulge such fantasies with impunity, for the fantasy of an oedipal victory must call forth the terrifying fantasy of the father's retribution. Gulliver tries to short-circuit this process by seeming to deny retroactively what, in his fantasy, he believes to have taken place—his triumph over the father. Moreover, he tries to assert the very *opposite* of his fantasy belief by claiming that his actions have been a "service" to the father. Let us look again at the relevant passage:

> It was now Day-light, and I returned to my House, without
> waiting to congratulate with the emperor; because, although I
> had done a very eminent Piece of Service, yet I could not tell
> how his Majesty might resent the Manner by which I had per-
> formed it: For, by the fundamental Laws of the Realm, it is Cap-
> ital in any Person, of what Quality soever, to make water within
> the Precincts of the Palace. (1.5.40)

We have already analyzed this passage as an example of Gulliver's
disingenuousness about his own masochism: only at the very end
of the episode does he acknowledge having committed a capital
offense, and he still claims not to know how the emperor might
resent it. But when we look at the passage in light of the oedipal
fantasy Gulliver is indulging, his disingenuousness takes on an
even darker cast. The "fundamental Laws of the Realm" that
Gulliver mentions as an afterthought refer here, in fact, to the
incest taboo—a law that, in the human psyche, does not allow for
extenuating circumstances. So Gulliver, at the surface level of his
explanation, puts on a front of naïveté and claims not to understand what he has done. We may assume, however, that at the
unconscious level Gulliver knows perfectly well what crime he has
committed, and hence we see unconscious irony in the phrases
"congratulate with the emperor," "a very eminent Piece of Service," and "could not tell how his Majesty might resent." The
irony results from the fact that Gulliver, at one level, is saying
more or less the opposite of what he believes to be the case. But
what purpose does the irony serve here? Is it merely the "big lie"
uttered in self-defense—"big" in the sense that it does not simply
deny a particular fact (as in, "I did *not* do you harm") but exag-
geratedly asserts the opposite of this fact ("I did you a very eminent service")? No, irony involves more than simply lying and
more than simply defense. There would be no irony here if the
phrases we have pointed to did not also serve a hidden aggressive
purpose, a purpose that in the present passage lies at the deepest
unconscious level. If Gulliver wants the emperor to congratulate
him on what Gulliver believes to be an oedipal victory over the
emperor-father himself, then he is asking the emperor to acknowledge defeat in a singularly humiliating manner: Congratulations
on your victory over me and your success with my wife the
empress—I will say that you have done me a service, for which I
certainly can have no wish to retaliate against you. Gulliver's
irony here involves two layers of defense (the lie being told at the

literal level and the fact that this lie is unconscious) and a layer of aggression, and it is intimately connected with the oedipal struggle he is engaged in.

In the male child's oedipal fantasies, the father knows perfectly well what the son is up to, and so in the version of these fantasies that lies behind the plot of part 1, the emperor of Lilliput is not taken in by Gulliver's defenses. Gulliver may protest his innocence all he wants—and this he certainly does when he retells the story and tries to justify himself to his readers—but the emperor demands that Gulliver be punished for his crime of incest and for his treasonous intentions against the emperor. The punishment is to be precisely what it was in the story of Oedipus himself: blindness as a substitute for death. In Freudian theory, of course, the blindness stands for castration, the mutilation of another valued organ; and this connection is at least hinted at in "A Voyage to Lilliput" by the fact that in his secret pocket Gulliver keeps a pair of spectacles as well as the "other little Conveniences." We recall, too, that almost from the beginning of part 1 Gulliver has been obsessed with protecting his eyes from injury, and at his most aggressive moment, when he steals the fleet of the Blefuscudians, his only real fear is the threat to his eyes.

But Gulliver's story and Oedipus's diverge at a crucial point, for whereas Oedipus acquiesces in the punishment for his crime, and even executes it on himself, Gulliver regards his punishment as undeserved and works to evade it. And yet Gulliver is, in the fantasy that lies behind part 1, guilty of exactly the same crime that Oedipus commits; the only difference is that Oedipus's incest is presented in terms of adult sexuality, whereas Gulliver—though ostensibly an adult—acts out the perverse notions that belong to infantile sexuality. Gulliver, in other words, has earned his punishment, too. This is a conclusion that everything in part 1 attempts to avoid. Gulliver himself tells his story in such a way that the emperor cannot with any justice punish him, even if technically he has broken a law. And Swift cooperates by presenting Gulliver's story as a satire on the injustice of kings in general—as if the book were primarily treating a realistic issue in political philosophy. In a way, of course, it is. But the political philosophy is a sublimation; and here as elsewhere in *Gulliver's Travels* Swift presents not only the sublimation but also the infantile fantasy from which it derives, and he gives us the opportunity of inspecting the connection between the two. The child "knows" he has committed a crime for which the father will punish him with castration or death, yet the child can bear neither the knowledge of his own guilt nor his fear of the punishment he believes he has earned. He half-solves his problem by repressing his guilt, though he still believes that the father will retaliate; his own innocence is then confirmed and his hostility to the father justified by his belief in the father's irrationality and injustice. Later, the adult comes to believe in the irrationality and injustice of kings and all those who represent the father to him; reality supplies him with all the evidence he needs to confirm his belief. This rational, adult belief aids him in repressing his unconscious, infantile belief in his own guilt toward the father, and it bolsters his certainty of his own innocence.

When Gulliver, unlike Oedipus, asserts his innocence and evades punishment at the hands of the emperor of Lilliput, he can do so only by paying a price of another kind. During the oedipal period the child falls prey to terrible conflicts, because so long as he (in the case of the male child) desires the mother, he will anxiously anticipate punishment by the father. Of course, even if the father senses the child's wishes and feels competitive toward the child, he will not ordinarily retaliate in the way the child fears. If the child can tolerate his desires, his guilt, and his irrational fears, then eventually—usually with the help of the parents—he learns to repress his unrealizable desires for the mother and to identify with the father in such a way that he represses his hostility toward the father. If, on the other hand, he cannot accomplish this developmental task, cannot tolerate the anxieties of the oedipal period, then often he will return psychologically to the relationships of an earlier period. This return, or regression, is of course an escape from present anxieties, but it costs the individual dearly, since it retards or precludes further development. Gulliver falls into this trap. He does not stand his ground in Lilliput, but driven by the threat of punishment he seeks a more just father, the emperor of Blefuscu. But to the guilty child trying to establish his innocence, there can be no just fathers. The emperor of Blefuscu offers Gulliver "his gracious Protection, if I would continue in his Service; wherein although I believed him sincere, yet I resolved never more to put any Confidence in Princes or Ministers, where I could possibly avoid it" (1.8.61). The same conflicts that were awakened in Lilliput could only arise in Blefuscu as well, as is confirmed for Gulliver when his resolution to depart is applauded by the emperor and the court of Blefuscu. So Gulliver escapes even more definitively: back to England first, but ultimately to the reprehensible servility and passivity of his existence in Brobdingnag. Unable to negotiate the perils of the oedipal period, Gulliver begins the regression whose ultimate price is the self-hatred and self-alienation that become pathologically evident at the end of part 4.

Regression is, indeed, the fundamental action of *Gulliver's Travels*. It characterizes, first of all, the plot line that runs through the voyages to Lilliput, Brobdingnag, and the Houyhnhnms—the three parts in which is played out the essential development of the book as a whole. We also see this regression in the frame story that is activated at the beginning and end of each part. Gulliver's wife and children and his life in England represent adult (genital) sexuality and the burdens of adulthood, and his repeated flights from his home give further evidence that something is holding him back from achieving psychological maturity. This something seems to be Gulliver's (Swift's) failure to tolerate the fears and desires of the oedipal period or to accomplish the necessary developmental tasks—despite, or perhaps because of, the persistence of infantile megalomaniacal fantasies that would seem to ease the anxieties of the oedipal period. The failure to deal with these anxieties leads to a surrender to passive, masochistic wishes, a surrender that itself brings on massive self-loathing from which Gulliver attempts to escape through false and ultimately even pathological identifications. So the solutions to which Gulliver resorts do not work; they only lead him away from any healthy adaptation and into a deeper state of psychological regression. When we leave Gulliver at the end of part 4, he can no longer tolerate his own self-contempt and so has projected the hated parts of himself onto his fellow humans; of course he can scarcely bear the sight of these creatures who mirror to him his own nature.

This, roughly, is the psychological action that lies at the base of *Gulliver's Travels*. To be sure, at the same time that Swift presents this action, he tries to draw our attention away from it and onto "higher" matters. But secretly he also wants us to inspect the infantile fears, fantasies, and wishes that run throughout the book. Swift is like the Gulliver who lovingly tells us about his bowel movements but does so with such apparent squeamishness and fastidiousness that he invites us to interpret him thus: Pay no attention to these low details which (for very suspicious reasons) I am obliged to recite; or in his own words, "I would not have dwelt so long upon a Circumstance, that perhaps at first Sight may appear not very momentous; if I had not thought it necessary to justify my Character in Point of Cleanliness to the World" (1.2.13). So even though Swift seems to direct his readers to such questions as "What is the nature of human reason?"—and we generally use these questions to teach the book—he also presents in full detail a psychological action that allows us to draw inferences about the psychological state in which the book originates. Having examined these psychological underpinnings, we may now ask how they are related to the irony for which the book is justly celebrated.

THE IRONY OF *GULLIVER'S TRAVELS*

In accounting for Swift's use of irony and other indirections in *Gulliver's Travels*, Swift's biographer Irvin Ehrenpreis quite naturally emphasizes the dangers that attended the publication of any political writings that might be construed as libellous or seditious. Ehrenpreis recalls that, from the time of his retirement from politics in 1714, Swift had written a number of pieces, some unfinished, in which he set down his views of English politics and of the events he had witnessed during his association with the Oxford-Bolingbroke ministry under Queen Anne—but that none of these efforts could be published during those years. For Ehrenpreis, Swift hit upon the idea of a fantastic voyage as a way of overcoming the de facto censorship that was frustrating his efforts at expression: "Thus the self-transforming energy of the unprintable essays found a new vehicle, bold enough to satisfy Swift's anger, expressive enough to convey his doctrine, but so disguised that it could be sold in London."[15] He also speaks of "Swift's wish to hide what he was doing from the profane while revealing it to the initiate."[16]

Ehrenpreis's view is not universally accepted. In his book *The Politics of "Gulliver's Travels,"* F. P. Lock argues that, although Swift claimed that the publication of his *Travels* would be dangerous, "this was probably more a reflection of what Swift liked to believe was the Whig government's repressive censorship than of the real state of affairs."[17] Lock cites, for example, the conclusion drawn by Donald Thomas on the basis of a study of the King's

Bench indictments: "Political censorship of the press between 1702 and 1730 is haphazard rather than systematic, according to the evidence of the indictments. Arrest and harassment of publishers, rather than full-scale prosecution, appears as the preferred method by which governments dealt with their critics."[18] Lock also claims that the government would never have risked a prosecution for seditious libel against *Gulliver's Travels,* because whether the action was successful or not, the government would only have looked foolish and would have increased the book's notoriety. On the contrary, he says, Walpole's general policy was to ignore the abusive attacks in the press and concentrate on the real sources of his power: the approval of the king and the House of Commons. Ehrenpreis's view that irony could afford Swift much-needed protection is vulnerable from another direction as well. Lennard J. Davis, relying on Francis Holt's study *The Law of Libel* (1818), concludes, "Even the use of irony and sarcasm, which cannot actually be said to be part of the direct content of a work, could constitute libel if such use maliciously attempted to encourage scandal."[19]

But even if Ehrenpreis is right to stress the dangers that Swift's opinions, expressed openly and without disguise, could have subjected him to, the dangers that Swift was evading—as we have stressed before—were not all realistic legal dangers, and the laws and politics of early eighteenth-century Britain cannot fully account for Swift's characteristic resort to irony. For evidence we need only look at an example such as the following letter in which Swift writes privately to his friend John Gay, on a subject not within the purview of political censorship. Apparently neither Swift nor Gay had written to the other since Swift's departure from England in 1714, until Gay sent a letter dated December 27, 1722. Swift began his reply:

> Coming home after a Short Christmas Ramble, I found a Letter upon my Table, and little expected when I opened it to read your Name at the Bottom. The best and greatest part of my Life till these last eight years I Spent in England, there I made my Friendships and there I left my Desires; I am condemned for ever to another Country, what is in Prudence to be done? I think to be oblitusq; meorum obliviscendus et illis; what can be the Design of your Letter but Malice, to wake me out of a Scurvy Sleep, which however is better than none, I am towards nine years older Since I left you Yet that is the least of my Alter-

ations: My Business, my Diversions my Conversations are all
entirely changed for the Worse, and So are my Studyes and my
Amusements in writing; Yet after all, this humdrum way of Life
might be passable enough if you would let me alone, I shall not
be able to relish my Wine, my Parsons, my Horses nor my Garden for three Months, till the Spirit you have raised Shall be dis-
possessed.[20]

The rhetorical approach to irony, implicit in Ehrenpreis's comments, must always trace its use either to the wish to avoid political censorship or to the wish to produce a memorable effect on
the listener. In the letter quoted there can be no question of political censorship. Nor, in my view, do we have here merely a titillat-
ing effect produced by substituting a shockingly rude insult for
the compliment hidden below it. There is simply too much feeling, too much accusation in that word "Malice" for it ever to
become transparent to another, deeper meaning. Perhaps we can
most easily see what is going on in this passage if we think of
another context in which such language might be intended
absolutely literally and without any extra, ironical meanings.
Imagine two former lovers: the woman broke off the relationship
years ago and has gone about her life, while the man, though he
has "forgotten" the affair, has never taken up with another
woman. She writes him a letter out of the blue, and these are the
sentiments she awakens in him. He knows she did not write out of
malice; but she has been negligent, for if she had considered his
feelings, she would have remained silent. Swift is, of course, exaggerating in claiming such sentiments, but still there is something
unequal in the relationship between him and Gay that faintly
embitters Swift's feelings. Because Swift needs Gay more than vice
versa, he bristles a little at the casualness with which Gay can
decide to correspond after eight years. Obviously these feelings
are not the main thing Swift is consciously trying to express in his
response to Gay; instead he is paying Gay an elaborate compliment through the use of ironic exaggeration and ironic blame:
you are so important to me that a letter from you will disrupt my
life for three months, so you ought to have left me alone. But the
exaggeration and the accusation that constitute the irony have
themselves a real basis in Swift's feelings; they do not derive from
some formulaic or mechanical method for creating an ironic compliment. In short, one can hardly read this letter without concluding that the irony here is not a rhetorical device but a way of

expressing divergent meanings that could not otherwise be captured—and that it is a mode of expression necessary and characteristic for someone who could entertain such ambivalent feelings. A political or rhetorical explanation of Swift's irony, even in *Gulliver's Travels*, simply will not suffice.

Of all the themes that obsess Swift in *Gulliver's Travels*, one of the most memorable is the Houyhnhnms' prohibition against lying—saying the thing that is not. Yet Swift's obsession with truthfulness seems odd, not only in a work of fiction, but also in a work characterized by much ironic language. For irony (as we have discussed in chapter 1) seems to be a form of lying, or at least a form of "saying the thing that is not." I would argue, however, that Swift's irony in *Gulliver's Travels* is absolutely in the service of his obsession with truth telling. Irony allows him to express the truth, in some measure, even when fears and anxieties are simultaneously forcing him to conceal it.

Let us look at an example from part 1. After Gulliver has spoken up for a generous peace with Blefuscu and has subsequently received a visit from that nation's ambassadors, he hears a report "that *Flimnap* and *Bolgolam* had represented my Intercourse with those Ambassadors, as a Mark of Disaffection, from which I am sure my Heart was wholly free" (1.5.38). If one leaves out the phrase "I am sure," then the remark is simply a falsehood (whether conscious or unconscious), and in fact only a few lines later Gulliver reminds us of his disaffection: "The Reader may remember, that when I signed those Articles upon which I recovered my Liberty, there were some which I disliked on Account of their being too servile, neither could any thing but an extreme Necessity have forced me to submit" (1.5.39). However, with the phrase "I am sure," the sentence quoted becomes slightly ironic. Formally, the phrase adds a double reassurance that Gulliver knows the sentiments of his own heart. But since, in ordinary discourse, we assume that a person can speak authoritatively about her own feelings, Gulliver's reiteration that "I am sure" about them comes across as defensive and serves to introduce an element of doubt—as if Gulliver were admitting the possibility that he might not know his own feelings or that his heart were some kind of alien body of which he was simply a privileged, but perhaps inaccurate, observer. The doubleness here results from the fact that Gulliver is delivering a faint subtext that goes very much in the opposite direction from the overt and emphasized message ("wholly free"). And this doubleness is ironic, as opposed to simply mendacious, because Gulliver himself (whether consciously or unconsciously) is delivering both messages to his audience. But it is also important to notice that the "primary" subtext—and we have emphasized this point before—does not actually contradict the main overt message in the way that a falsehood contradicts, or is the negative of, a truthful statement. Gulliver simply admits covertly that there is a (seemingly insignificant) possibility that he might not know his own heart and that therefore his heart could harbor some disaffection of which he is not aware. Unconsciously and legalistically, he has protected himself from lying, and at the same time he has defended himself against any imputation of disloyalty, against the danger of the emperor's counterattack, and against his own guilt stemming from this disaffection. To get to the true opposite of the main overt message—that is, to the statement that Gulliver's heart was filled with disaffection—one has to perform a second translation, not just moving from the overt to the "primary" covert message but translating as well the understatement of the latter; the slim possibility of disaffection becomes the certainty of rebellion. But this unconscious ironic meaning, however obscured for defensive reasons, also belongs to Gulliver's statement.

Ehrenpreis draws attention to the parallel between the sentence we have just analyzed and a sentence in Swift's tract *An Enquiry into the Behaviour of the Queen's Last Ministry*. For Ehrenpreis, this parallel illustrates "how deeply the story of Gulliver reflected the experience of the author."[21] But a comparison of the two passages also shows us how close we come, in *Gulliver's Travels*, to the psychological underpinnings of Swift's irony. Though it was not published until 1765, Swift began the *Enquiry* in 1715 shortly after three of his friends, leaders of the Tory government that had collapsed following the accession of George I in 1714, had been accused by Parliament of high treason; two of them, the duke of Ormonde and Henry St. John, viscount Bolingbroke, had fled to France, while Robert Harley, earl of Oxford, was awaiting trial in the Tower of London.[22] Swift writes:

> And here I cannot but lament my own particular Misfortune, who having singled out three Persons from among the rest of Mankind, on whose Friendship and Protection I might depend; whose Conversation I most valued, and chiefly confined my self

to, should live to see them all within the Compass of a Year, accused of high Treason; two of them attainted, and in Exile, and the third under his Tryall, whereof God knows what may be the Issue. As my own Heart was free from all treasonable Thoughts, so I did little Imagine my self to be perpetually in the Company of Traytors.[23]

Here we see that Swift, writing a political pamphlet, does not dare suggest that he might be less than perfectly knowledgeable about his own heart, and he states simply and unambiguously that "my own Heart was free from all treasonable Thoughts." His daringly ambiguous irony he now directs against his friends. (Here the ironic meaning is not a subtle adjustment to the overt and unironic message; rather, the ironic meaning is the apparent principal meaning of the last sentence quoted.) Swift obviously wishes the reader to infer that no friends of Swift could be traitors, because the loyal Swift would never associate with people who were. Logically, however, the reader need not draw this conclusion from what Swift says. Swift actually affirms only this: that a perfectly loyal man cannot imagine treacherous thoughts in the company around him. Such an affirmation says nothing about the loyalty of these other people. If Swift had wanted to write ironically but with logical consequence about the loyalty of his friends, he could easily have chosen a more appropriate protasis: When I saw the great services that my friends performed daily for their country, I did little imagine myself to be perpetually in the company of traitors. But obviously the major idea that Swift, unconsciously, is trying to get across here concerns not the loyalty of his friends but his own innocence. Undoubtedly at the deepest level he means exactly what he says here: Even if my friends are traitors, I would not have been aware of their treachery because of my own innocence, so do not transfer onto me your judgment that they are guilty.

What we want to notice, in comparing the sentences from *Gulliver's Travels* and the *Enquiry*, is the relation between Swift's "I" and the kind of irony he uses. In the *Enquiry*, where the "I" is more or less the author Swift, the irony serves specific offensive and defensive purposes, and it is directed away from the speaker. Either Swift's irony is a way of sacrificing his friends to protect himself, or it may even be an unconscious attack on his friends. (He may have unconsciously suspected—as was indeed the case—

that Oxford and Bolingbroke had more dealings with James Edward Stuart, the pretender to the British throne, than they were willing to discuss with Swift, dealings that would indeed leave them open to the charge of treason.) On the other hand, in *Gulliver's Travels* Swift expresses an almost identical sentiment but does so in a fictional context where the "I" is itself mixed up with a fictional persona. In this context the irony seems to have a much less sharply defined function. In fact, it begins to undermine the speaker's own self-protective assertions and even his sense of himself. It leaves the speaker unpleasantly exposed. We have suggested that, in this example, irony allows Gulliver-Swift to speak in accordance with an obsession with truthfulness, but the truth that is allowed a modicum of expression here is one that does the speaker no good and that the speaker would rather conceal. The unconscious irony has a distinct masochistic undertone. It also reflects ambivalence and conflicts of the oedipal period.

Let us go a bit further in generalizing about the contrast between the two passages we have looked at. Let us say that the passages point to the two main directions in which irony can move—and hence to the two kinds of psychological explanation which irony invites. In the *Enquiry* sentence, the irony serves to defend Swift's idealized friends in Queen Anne's ministry (the idealization is evident in the descriptions of the ministers that precede and follow the quoted passage). But it also allows Swift to attack these friends covertly. So the irony reflects ambivalence toward idealized—that is, oedipal—figures, and the expression of this ambivalence is a simultaneous defense and attack. One might argue that the true unconscious purpose is the attack and that only fear prevents this attack from being made directly and unambiguously—that the irony serves primarily as a defensive cover. This is the kind of argument that W. N. Evans, for example, makes about irony.[24] Such an argument is essentially a psychological version of the political-rhetorical model of irony, and it shares with the latter a major defect: it invests the essence of an ironic statement's meaning in only one of the levels of meaning we discern in it. This disproportion does not adequately reflect our experience of irony. In the sentence we are analyzing, Swift's ironic way of expressing his overt defense of his friends has allowed him also to give vent to a covert (though literal) attack; but we scarcely doubt the sincerity of his defense. In short, we would do better to connect irony with psychological ambivalence.

This connection itself invites two further steps: first, ambivalence (in Freudian theory) is the hallmark of the obsessive-compulsive neurosis, which is therefore also implicated in irony; and, second, ambivalence derives from an inability to resolve the divergent trends of the oedipal period (represented in the positive and negative oedipal complexes), so that we should also be able to find representatives of these trends in the psychological milieu in which we find irony. We have already suggested ways in which *Gulliver's Travels* exhibits these various psychological traits, and we will return to this point shortly.

The kind of irony we have just been speaking of we might call "other-directed." We have used an example from outside of *Gulliver's Travels* as a way of establishing the contrast, but we could easily point to innumerable instances within the work itself. This is the kind of irony that comes closest to the public irony of rhetorical textbooks, and appropriately we have taken our example from one of Swift's political tracts. As suggested in the section "Three Paradigms of Irony" (chap. 1), however, the other-directedness of even the most "impersonal" irony is far from absolute. An analysis of the *Enquiry* example, or virtually any other, would show that irony is always a double-edged sword and that it always exacts a certain price from the speaker herself. But whereas this price might not be very evident in the more public, rhetorical forms of irony, it becomes the paramount characteristic of a second familiar kind of irony, which we might call "self-directed"; this is irony that the speaker uses at his own expense, even if it also seems directed at an outer target—irony, in other words, that has the strong odor of masochism. To be sure, all irony has at least in part a masochistic purpose, but often this purpose is fairly well disguised, so that the aggressive purpose is more prominent. Bergler's theories provide a telling explanation of this phenomenon: Psychic masochism is so repugnant to the superego that it must be concealed by an overlay of "pseudo-aggression," which—even if a punishable offense—is a lesser crime to the superego than is masochism. Nonetheless, the superego's strictures against overt masochism are often violated in one way or another; the common phenomenon of self-deprecating irony would simply be one instance of this fact, though one of particular interest in the present context.

It would seem that, in *Gulliver's Travels*, we cannot really speak of any extreme form of "self-directed" irony. Everywhere the irony seems to fit too closely into the other paradigm I have sketched: aggressive attacks against hated (but perhaps also idealized) oedipal figures. But there is considerable ambiguity in one instance, and that is in the irony directed against Gulliver. For when Swift makes his own "I" the target of irony, there is bound to be a certain amount of psychic ambiguity; every "I" Swift utters cannot fail to include Swift himself in some fashion or other.[25] The confusion is perhaps clearest in the "Letter from Capt. Gulliver, to his Cousin Sympson," added to later additions of *Gulliver's Travels*. Gulliver laments that "instead of seeing a full Stop put to all Abuses and Corruptions, at least in this little Island, as I had Reason to expect: Behold, after above six Months Warning, I cannot learn that my Book hath produced one single Effect according to mine Intentions" (xxxiv). Swift is being ironical here about Gulliver's naïve "actual" intentions in writing, but the critique would apply just as well to Swift, the author behind the author, if we consider that in Swift's view the only possible purpose of a satirical work would be to improve humankind. Swift may not be so innocent as to believe that his work *will* lead to improvements, but he recognizes that, logically, such a hope has to count as the implicit intention of his work. So Swift obviously includes his own "I" here as victim of the ironical thrust. The two "I"s—Swift's and Gulliver's—approach very near to one another, because each of the two "I"s appears as the author of the present book.

Elsewhere there is more distance between them, and the distance is precisely the function of the fictional context that irony always seems to build up—a fictional context that allows a statement to be both true and false at the same time. Consider the following sentence in the "Voyage to Brobdingnag": "I walked with Intrepidity five or six Times before the very Head of the Cat, and came within half a Yard of her; whereupon she drew her self back, as if she were more afraid of me" (2.1.75). In the fictional context of Brobdingnag, the sentiments Gulliver expresses here are perfectly just. He *does* show intrepidness in walking in front of the cat, for which he would be entitled to some part of the admiration he seems to be claiming here. But what makes this sentence ironic is the fact that neither Swift nor the reader can entirely hold on to this fictional context. It has a tendency to disappear for a moment, so that we imagine this "I" as an ordinary person walking "within half a Yard" of a cat and demanding admiration for his bravery in doing so. Therefore, in so far as the fictional context is forgotten, the author is making an ironic negation of the speaker's claim. But we can go further. If we remove the fictional context even more completely, by assimilating the speaker to the author (so that the "I" represents Swift himself) and performing the necessary abstractions, we can see that the irony here is actually self-directed. In fact, we are given an ironic self-portrait of Swift the ironist: that is to say, of someone who makes a show of bravado when he is not really in any danger. (To make such a statement about himself, the ironist both asserts the danger and ironically denies it.) Moreover, in the last part of the sentence quoted, we see, faintly, the complicated connection between the intrepidness-timidity of the ironist and the untested megalomania that we found to be so significant in part 1. Since the ironist attacks, he may attribute his immunity from counterattack either to his own power or to the putative—in fact, projected—fear that he awakens in his object. However, the real reason for the lack of a counterattack may actually derive from the defenses with which an ironic attack is always hedged—or even from the fecklessness of the ironist. The ironist never actually tests his strength against the target of his attack, but in his megalomania he may assume that he is an awe-inspiring opponent. In the present example, Gulliver begins his walk in front of the cat only after he concludes: "it happened there was no Danger; for the Cat took not the least Notice of me when my Master placed me within three Yards of her" (2.1.75).

The major point here, then, is that much of the irony of *Gulliver's Travels* turns back on the speaker and, through him, ultimately on the actual author Swift. This is an odd conclusion to draw, but one confirmed in perhaps the most famous sentence Swift ever wrote, the first lines of the Latin epitaph he included in his will: "Hic depositum est corpus *Jonathan Swift*, S.T.D. hujus ecclesiae cathedralis decani, ubi saeva indignatio ulterius cor lacerare nequit" [Here is laid the body of Jonathan Swift, S.T.D., dean of this cathedral church, where savage indignation can no longer lacerate (his) heart].[26] We think of Swift as lashing *others* with his fierce anger, but here Swift admits that he himself was the one torn most mercilessly by its violence (although, unconsciously, even this admission is itself partly denied, since Latin style does not require Swift to identify the lacerated heart as specifically his). Swift's anger—and the irony that was one expression of it—served ultimately a masochistic purpose.

I don't think we can enquire much further here into why masochistic anger should be so basic to Swift's psychology. We would get bogged down either in (inevitably circular) biographical speculation or in the ultimate questions of psychoanalytic theory that cannot be further advanced in a work of this scope—questions, that is, about the ultimate source of human aggressiveness. But we can usefully expand on Bergler's speculations as to what might *happen* to such masochistic anger. The masochism of this anger is intolerable, so the individual tries to direct it outward—either to prove to himself through a show of aggression (as Bergler theorizes) that he is not a masochist or simply to find a less painful way of expressing the anger. For this purpose the individual needs to find self-justifying provocations—injustices—of which life provides an abundance to anyone looking for them. Notice, for example, that in using the word *indignatio,* Swift implies that there is a legitimate outward cause for the anger—the indignation—that lacerates his heart.

The question remains as to why irony should be such a useful vehicle for expressing this kind of masochistic anger. The action of *Gulliver's Travels,* as we have sketched it here, may give us a clue. This action moves from an oedipal defeat to severe psychological regression—a regression that leads to self-hatred and self-condemnation and that is unavailingly countered by desperate identifications with admired adult figures. All these elements seem to be present in irony. First, the oedipal defeat is reflected in the ironist's inability to make a direct, overt attack on the adult authorities. Evans puts it this way:

> In a permissive home overt rebellion is easy and indeed often encouraged by the environment. In a strict household, however, where discipline is enforced and reinforced by the environment, overt rebellion is well-nigh impossible, as the forces aligned against the child are too great. If he engages in an open power struggle, he will lose. He has, therefore, to resort to other and subtler methods: irony is pre-eminently the weapon of the "well-brought up" child.[27]

Second, irony mimics a regression in that the ironist assumes the mask of a "naïf," as we usually say; the ironist puts away adult knowledge and makes herself into a kind of childlike innocent. Third, irony involves a pseudo-identification with the powerful figures whose opinions or precepts are repeated literally, though

at the same time these precepts are overthrown by the ironic subtext. On the basis of these similarities we might make further
inferences. We may speculate, in the direction of Bergler's argument, that the ironist who allows himself to be reduced to such
infantile helplessness in the face of the powerful adults directs his
primary anger not at these oppressors from his childhood (and
their successors) but at himself, precisely because he has given up
the prerogative of ever truly challenging, or becoming, an adult.
This primary anger is reflected very clearly—and this is the fourth
similarity we would point to between irony and the psychological
action of *Gulliver's Travels*—in the masochism and self-hatred
that come to dominate the psychological tone of the novel. Only
as a secondary result does the ironist unconsciously try to direct
this anger outward—as a way of proving to himself that he is not
that which he very well knows he is. But this secondary attack on
the figures of authority never transcends the psychological condition in which it arises; it must always be a disguised, ambivalent,
and defense-minded attack. Whatever the ironist's megalomania
may lead him to think about the omnipotence of his attacks, their
ironic form makes them much less a test of the ironist's power
than they might seem—just as Gulliver, in part 1, fears to provoke
any true test of his superiority to the Lilliputians. The ironic statement always contains its own escape hatch—especially including
the basic pose that the ironist is too much the innocent child to
know what she is saying.

IRONY AND IDEALS IN *GULLIVER'S TRAVELS*

Gulliver's Travels allows us to investigate one further problem in
the psychological genesis of irony, and that is the relation between
irony and ideals. To approach this problem, let us first recall
Wayne Booth's well-known distinction, developed throughout *A
Rhetoric of Irony*, between "stable" and "unstable" irony. For
Booth, irony is stable when the reader can translate from the surface meaning of an ironic statement back to some hidden, more or
less opposed meaning that lends itself to a definite formulation.
This is the irony of the rhetorical tradition, and it is contrasted
with the irony of romanticism and beyond, where often no positive statement can be readily inferred from the ironic communication; we know only what is being rejected. Swift, of course, ought

to fall well within the rhetorical tradition of stable irony. Individual ironic statements in *Gulliver's Travels* are, as a rule, readily
translatable, and we sense throughout the book the existence of
passionate beliefs that serve as the standpoint for the various
ironic critiques. But when we come to actually define these beliefs,
we often experience more difficulty than we expected, primarily
because, when we perform the various translations necessary to
get back to Swift's actual beliefs, the results of these translations
do not always harmonize very well with one another. The suppos-
edly stable ironies often add up to a great deal of instability—an
instability that is perhaps best reflected in the long-standing and
seemingly irresolvable critical dispute over the meaning of part 4,
"A Voyage to the Country of the Houyhnhnms."

It is my contention that the difficulty we have in establishing
Swift's beliefs in *Gulliver's Travels*—or rather, his ideals, as I
would prefer to say—is inevitable, given the psychological determinants of verbal irony. As we have seen, irony can be shown to
have roots deep in the unconscious; and the ironist, in giving way
to his penchant for irony, opens up a path by which the unconscious fears, desires, and ambivalences of childhood can achieve
at least partial expression. Of these unconscious emotions, one of
the most important to emerge in ironic discourse is what Freudi-
ans would see as the inevitable human ambivalence toward one's
own ideals. This ambivalence lies behind the contradictions and
confusions that have led us in so many directions as readers of
Gulliver's Travels; and indeed, the equally inevitable attempt to
resolve this ambivalence is enacted by Gulliver in part 4 of the
satire.

Before turning to the Houyhnhnms, let us first look at a relatively simple and straightforward example of the kind of contradiction that troubles our reading of *Gulliver's Travels*. The king of
Brobdingnag, in his long reply to Gulliver's account of manners
and morals in England, seems in many respects a mouthpiece for
Swift's own considered views; so rational, moderate, and com-
monsensical are the king's opinions that we naturally assume that
they are endorsed by the author, even without external evidence.
For example, on the question of religious differences, the king
responds to Gulliver as follows:

> He laughed at my odd Kind of Arithmetick (as he was pleased
> to call it) in reckoning the Numbers of our People by a Compu-

tation drawn from the several Sects among us in Religion and Politicks. He said, he knew no Reason, why those who entertain Opinions prejudicial to the Publick should be obliged to change, or should not be obliged to conceal them. And, as it was Tyranny in any Government to require the first, so it was Weakness not to enforce the second: For, a Man may be allowed to keep Poisons in his Closet, but not to vend them about as Cordials. (2.6.115)

In the case of this particular passage, we can even find external evidence that the king's opinion represents Swift's conscious beliefs. Thus, in his "Thoughts on Religion," Swift writes:

Liberty of conscience, properly speaking, is no more than the liberty of possessing our own thoughts and opinions, which every man enjoys without fear of the magistrate: But how far he shall publicly act in pursuance of those opinions, is to be regulated by the laws of the country. Perhaps, in my own thoughts, I prefer a well-instituted commonwealth before a monarchy; and I know several others of the same opinion. Now, if, upon this pretence, I should insist upon liberty of conscience, form conventicles of republicans, and print books, preferring that government, and condemning what is established, the magistrate would, with great justice, hang me and my disciples. It is the same case in religion, although not so avowed, where liberty of conscience, under the present acceptation, equally produces revolutions, or at least convulsions and disturbances in a state. [28]

However, when Swift is being ironic, he seems to contradict the moderate position expressed by the king. In part 1, Gulliver repeats the history of the religious disputes raging for four generations in Lilliput and Blefuscu between the Big-Endians and their opponents. Here is an excerpt from that history:

It is allowed on all Hands, that the primitive Way of breaking Eggs before we eat them, was upon the larger End: But his present Majesty's Grand-father, while he was a Boy, going to eat an Egg, and breaking it according to the ancient Practice, happened to cut one of his Fingers. Whereupon the Emperor his Father, published an Edict, commanding all his Subjects, upon great Penalties, to break the smaller End of their Eggs. The People so highly resented this Law, that our Histories tell us, there have been six Rebellions raised on that Account; wherein one Emperor lost his Life, and another his Crown. These civil Commotions were constantly fomented by the Monarchs of *Ble-*

fuscu; and when they were quelled, the Exiles always fled for Refuge to that Empire. It is computed, that eleven Thousand Persons have, at several Times, suffered Death, rather than submit to break their Eggs at the smaller End. (1.4.33)

Any reader would feel this passage to be "ironic," but we need to ask first of all whether the irony here can be grounded in the kind of concrete verbal irony which we have insisted on making the prototype for our definition of irony. To answer this question, we should recall from our various analyses that irony inevitably involves repeating the opinion of some other person. The "other person," however, tends to be one of two opposite sorts: either the childlike, innocent naïf or the adult authority figure (sometimes the collective adult authority of received opinion). In either case, the ironist *seems* to be identifying himself totally with this other figure; he is the naïf whose innocent views are being expressed, or he acquiesces completely in the views he is mouthing that belong, in fact, to the authorities. The ironist is obviously well protected in both cases. As an innocent child, he is not responsible for adult reinterpretations of his words and motives. As a spokesman for the authorities, he leaves them no grounds to suspect him of treason and rebellion. When irony is conscious, the ironist is aware that the alien opinions he is repeating are not identical with his "real" opinions. When irony is unconscious, the ironist believes himself totally identified with the views he is expressing, but he conveys through various signals his secret, unconscious contempt for them. Finally, we have noted that the only significant difference between literary irony and this model of everyday irony is that in literature the unified ironist may split herself up into her various components.

In the present passage, we note that the ideas being expressed (or directly implied) do not, in point of fact, belong to Gulliver at all. The section is actually a long passage in indirect discourse, with Gulliver reporting the words of Reldresal, the principal secretary of private affairs in Lilliput. At some points in the secretary's discourse we are reminded grammatically that we are hearing indirect speech, but in the sentences quoted here, such reminders are almost totally lacking. Thus, Gulliver appears to adopt the secretary's words as his own. We can easily see the connection between the ironic structure of this passage and the structure of ordinary verbal irony. Reldresal's words belong to adult authority, and they are repeated without alteration and without comment by the innocent Gulliver, who does not see the absurdity of the facts and values embedded in these words. Swift has, in fact, combined the two possible alien voices that are heard in ordinary ironic speech—the voice of the naïf and that of the adult authority; such a combination is, of course, also possible in everyday irony. At the same time Swift, through exaggeration and antithesis, points out the absurdity of the basic opinion implied by the secretary's history: that the present state of affairs, though bad, arose for reasons in themselves good and sufficient. The reader understands that Swift cannot share this opinion, and through further interpretation of the exaggerated allegory the reader also applies Swift's dissent to the official account of the rise of Protestantism in England.

At the very least, we have here an instance where Swift's ironic meanings (in the present passage) seem to contradict his direct meanings (as expressed in the above speech by the king of Brobdingnag); in the king's speech, Swift accepts the right of authority to require public observance of religious and political orthodoxy, whereas in Gulliver's speech he questions this right on the grounds of arbitrariness and cruelty. One might, of course, try to explain away this contradiction in various ways. For example, one might argue that, in imagining a dispute over how properly to break an egg, Swift is alluding only to the relatively insignificant theological differences that were often blown way out of proportion—to theological hair-splitting, as it were—and not to the truly important issues that divided Anglicans from Catholics and Dissenters. And indeed, in doctrinal matters Swift argued vigorously against oversubtlety, which he saw as fomenting needless dissensions. But Swift's allegory does not really admit the possibility of other, more important points of dispute; the proper way to break an egg becomes the founding doctrine of the Lilliputian religion and the origin of Lilliput's dispute with Blefuscu. However much we would like to avoid accusing Swift of self-contradiction, he seems indeed to be guilty of it—although his irony serves its usual defensive purpose and requires us to do considerable interpretation before filing our brief, and the ironist, of course, can always repudiate our "interpretations."

In his biography of Swift, Irvin Ehrenpreis takes up a similar problem when he tries to explain how Swift, in *Gulliver's Travels,* could seem to support beliefs so much at odds with the tenor of his life and other works. Ehrenpreis proposes the thesis that Swift held a "general, moral outlook" that could conflict with the specific "historical positions" that he took up.[29] Ehrenpreis implies what we are getting in *Gulliver's Travels* are the general principles, even when they conflict with the principles that could be deduced from Swift's own practice; thus, in his satire, Swift implies that religious and political differences are relatively insignificant, whereas in practice he was a vigorous and combative partisan. Swift, Ehrenpreis argues, did not worry about inconsistency; caught up in the excitement of an argument or a topic, he would pursue it wherever it took him, without worrying about any overall system. Indeed, in one important instance, Ehrenpreis even finds inconsistency within *Gulliver's Travels* itself: "Absorbed in the depiction of the moral life, the life of reason, [Swift] represented the Houyhnhnms as dignified or awesome. Absorbed in the historical drama of his narrative, he let them appear limited and fallible."[30]

To his credit, Ehrenpreis does not try to minimize the contradictions he finds, and the explanation for them that he proposes is psychologically quite suggestive. And yet the theory doesn't really explain what most needs explanation: *Why* was Swift excited by arguments that tended to undermine his ordinary beliefs? Why was he borne off in these particular (conflicting) directions? What do the subversive arguments have to do with the ironic discourse in which they are expressed?

In an article focusing especially on the *Tale of a Tub*, Claude Rawson offers an argument that might indeed answer these questions. According to Rawson, Swift realizes, in part through introspection, that sectarianism and free thinking arise not solely out of moral badness but also out of "an innate mental perversity" that is "a psychological feature of the human condition, implicating all men, including ultimately Swift." Swift's solution to this dilemma is a "repudiating mimicry of the subversive intensities of the human mind."[31]

One virtue of Rawson's theory is that it would account for the emergence of subversive opinions in Swift's *ironic* writings, since irony can be seen precisely as a kind of "repudiating mimicry." In addition, the theory would explain why Swift's irony, far from being simply a rhetorical device for presenting his views, seems to arise from the very depths of Swift's psyche: irony becomes a way of exorcising the devils of doubt and rebellion by which Swift feels himself beset. But there are also problems with Rawson's theory. For one thing, it assumes that Swift remains in control of his own "innate mental perversity," so that any subversive intensities present in his work are there not as themselves but as a "repudiating mimicry." But if Swift is exerting this kind of control, then we should not find in a work like *Gulliver's Travels* the contradictions that we have been talking about. The other possibility, of course, is that Swift is actually indulging his own "innate mental perversity"—even if he doesn't realize that he is doing so or thinks that he is repudiating it. It is this latter possibility that I would like to explore here.

Let us put the question differently. Instead of asking why, in his ironic discourse, Swift seems to contradict beliefs that he elsewhere appears to uphold, let us ask whether any other outcome is possible. Could a positive statement of beliefs and ideals ever harmonize with an ironic statement?

From the rhetorical point of view, the answer is assuredly yes. In interpreting an ironic statement, one translates back from the surface meaning, not truly intended by the author, to the covert meaning, which is the one actually intended; and there is no reason why this covert meaning should differ in form or structure from a similar statement that was not originally hidden by an ironic overlay. But from a psychological point of view, we must reach a different conclusion. The psychological key lies in the relationship between the positive and negative aspects of the superego.

In its negative aspect, the superego is viewed by the ego as prohibitive and brutally punishing. It is the implacable instrument of justice that metes out retribution whenever the individual, even in fantasy, transgresses against its laws. The prohibition against incest would be an archetypal instance of the superego's laws, and, indeed, this law figures prominently in the plot of *Gulliver's Travels*: We have already seen how Gulliver's attempt to flee punishment for his fantasized incest precipitates his spiraling regression and prevents him from negotiating the oedipal crisis. The "real" punishment (of blindness and death) that Gulliver flees within the context of the novel's fantasy world represents the fantasied punishment with which the superego threatens the ego. But the superego has a more positive aspect as well. The superego also enforces upon the ego the individual's own ideals; it punishes the ego when the latter fails to live up to these ideals. (Psychoanalysts dispute whether these ideals reside in the ego or in the superego.

For our purposes the distinction is irrelevant and is, in fact, an example of how easily the two psychic agencies can be over-reified.) This aspect of the superego emerges, for example, in Bergler's theory that the superego requires the ego to exhibit active control and to avoid passive, masochistic behavior and that it threatens the ego with punishment if it violates this ideal. This more "positive" side of the superego also appears in *Gulliver's Travels*; as we have seen, Gulliver's pseudo-aggressiveness (e.g., against the Lilliputians, whom he never quite challenges despite his self-assurances that he could easily overpower them) can be analyzed as an attempt to deflect such a threat on the part of the superego.

The connection between these two aspects of the superego, the positive and the negative, is intimate, for both result from the child's attempt to take into herself something alien, something derived from the parental authorities who have coerced as well as nurtured her. This alien structure within the psyche is absolutely necessary, at the very least for self-protection, but it also presents its own dangers to the individual: the superego is capable of merciless and sadistic retaliation for the slightest infraction of its standards. The individual's ego must therefore be strong enough to protect itself from the onslaughts of the superego. Individuals protect themselves in various ways, of which a common, but ultimately rather unsatisfactory, one is what psychoanalysts call (following Anna Freud) "identification with the aggressor." In the present context, identification with the aggressor would mean putting away any conscious sense that the prohibitions and ideals enforced by the superego are in any way alien to the ego. But a total identification with the punitive superego is in fact impossible. Such an identification would deny not only the vital libidinal impulses but also any sense the individual has of possessing some irreducible center that is inalienably his. So even the individual who identifies with his punitive superego is bound to demur as well, at least on an unconscious level, and to insist that the superego's demands are in some ways foreign to him—and inappropriate and unjust. This ambivalent, and secret or quasi-secret, rebelliousness is the origin of irony. Sometimes the rebelliousness is directed against the rules and prohibitions laid down by parental (societal) authorities, and sometimes it is directed against the ideals derived from these same authorities. Sometimes the rebelliousness comes out more as an *ad hominem* attack against the authority figure himself (or his successors), and sometimes it is directed more at the abstract remnants of authority. Often the aggressiveness is conscious, and concealed only in a transparent (though, to the ironist, crucial) manner; sometimes it remains unconscious on the part of the ironist. But in whatever form it appears, irony is the sign that the ironist will not totally identify herself with that foreign element in herself made up of the prohibitions and ideals of parental authority. And since *all* prohibitions and ideals are descendants of those derived from the authorities of childhood, ultimately the ironist is actively resisting her own impulse to identify with any ideal or prohibition whatsoever. In other words, at the very moment when a person chooses to express himself ironically, he is exercising the ambivalent rebelliousness that precludes his full acceptance of the superego's authority and of any of its commands—an acceptance, indeed, that in many respects the ironist may devoutly wish to force upon himself.

Once we conceive of the genesis of irony in this manner, we can no longer hold on to any hard-and-fast distinction between "stable" and "unstable" irony. The infinite, or at least unstoppable, irony of some of the romantics becomes an extreme case of the instability that must inhere in all irony whose roots lie, not in the textbook practice of rhetoric, but in the fundamental psychic traits of the ironist. The difference in the irony of a book like *Gulliver's Travels* and of a romantic work like Lermontov's *Hero of Our Time* results not so much from differences in the nature of the irony itself as in differences in what surrounds the irony. As we see in the passages just quoted, Swift is likely to "say the same thing" both ironically and unironically—that is, in some relatively direct, overt fashion. The presence of these overt statements then gives us the illusion that a stable ground underlies the irony, a constant set of beliefs and ideals to which the ironic statements ultimately refer. But when, as in the two passages we have been analyzing, we have the chance to compare seemingly equivalent statements, we see that the ironic statement and the nonironic one are not always in sync. In the present case, indeed, we must consider the two statements as repeating, in their relationship to one another, the same ambivalence that we find within the ironic statement itself. The ironist pays obeisance to the very authorities, and their ideals, that he cannot help ridiculing whenever he feels himself sufficiently protected by his evanescent ironic smoke screen.

We can best understand the relationship Swift the ironist takes toward his own ideals by looking at the celebrated "Utopia" he creates in part 4 of *Gulliver's Travels*.[32] In this connection, let us first recall Reik's brilliant insight that an obsessional idea can take the form of an ironic statement that the obsessive utters over and over to himself, unaware of his own irony. Reik gives the example, discussed in chapter 1 above, of the young nobleman who obsessively repeated to himself the thought that servants and members of the lower classes were devils. Intellectually the young man understood that he did not believe this idea to be true, but he still could not free himself from its power over him. In fact, as Reik shows, the idea belonged not to the young man, but to his parents. However, this fact was not recognizable, because the idea was no longer in the form in which his parents had taught it to their son. The parents had taught, Be a good Christian and love thy neighbor; simultaneously they had taught a second message, Stay away from the servants. The young man had simply combined the two precepts and drawn the logical conclusion from their juxtaposition: If I am not to love servants, then they must not be my fellow human beings; and if they aren't human beings worthy of my love, then they must be devils. The crucial point here is that in mouthing the precepts of authority, the young man transforms them in such a way as to expose both their absurdity and his contempt for them. The transformation follows the ironist's typical maneuver: the ironist exaggerates an idea in such a way that the statement seems to be self-evidently false and, therefore, incapable of being credited even by the speaker herself. The particular exaggeration is also typical of irony—the ironist pushes an idea to its logical extremes (and beyond), putting it in more literal or graphic form than the idea can tolerate without exploding. Essentially, Reik's young patient has revealed his scorn for his parents' ideals by stating these beliefs in an ironic form—a form that indicates that he himself does not accept the beliefs. Yet because his contempt for his parents and for their precepts seems so dangerous to him, it remains unconscious, and he does not understand the true source of his obsessional idea. Indeed, the very fact that he still "believes" the obsessional idea, even though it is patently absurd, shows his inability to free himself from the parental ideals from which it is derived and for which he has such contempt. Though he, like every obsessive-compulsive neurotic, feels that the obsessional idea is something foreign to him—indeed it is, as the descendant of his parents' teaching—it continues to exercise control over him. And we may note in passing that Reik's obsessional patient torments *himself* with this ironic statement of his parents' beliefs; the authorities themselves are not directly attacked. This last result would seem to be directly opposed to the behavior typical of the ironist—except that, as we have seen with Swift, even relatively overt ironic attacks have a hidden masochistic purpose as well.

How, then, does Reik's obsessional patient afford us insight into Swift's depiction of the Houyhnhnms? The ideal represented in Houyhnhnmland—reason ruling over human behavior—is clear enough, and indeed Freudian theory specifically names this ideal as one likely to be resisted by the unconscious.[33] But Swift obscures his resistance to the ideal of reason by denying, through an elaborate double game, that he is making ironic statements about this ideal. Swift's strategy involves a reversal of the usual time sequence involved in irony whenever it is not an absolutely simultaneous event. Normally, that is, the ironist gives us first the straightforward statement (that will turn out to be ambiguously intended) and afterwards the additional remark that retroactively subverts the earlier statement. In part 4, however, Swift *begins* by providing the subversive information—that the speakers who will present the ideals of reason later in the book are in fact horses, brute animals whose "opinions" we would natually dissociate from the author's. But then, by having Gulliver's Houyhnhnm master speak with what seems like excellent common sense (so that we easily identify the Houyhnhnms' opinions as the author's), Swift effectively denies that he is using his horses to speak ironically. And yet Swift's denial is—purposely—fragile. Should we ever receive too striking a reminder, however brief, that a normally irrational creature is offering dicta about reason, then we would be bound to suspect these dicta of being ironic. Swift sets up a situation that would automatically produce ironic statements and then delivers in this situation statements that generally strike us as unironic. The result is twofold. On the one hand, by raising and then frustrating expectations of irony, Swift's implicit denial of ironic intent seems all the more deliberate and sincere. On the other hand, the expectations of irony, once raised, must be continuously suppressed, or they will easily gain the upper hand. Thus, the basic strategy Swift embarks on in part 4 already reveals a potentially ironic treatment of its ideals—but also involves a firm denial that there will be any such irony.

The suppression of irony in part 4 depends on two things: first, we must forget the "horseness" of the Houyhnhnms, and, second, the Houyhnhnms' beliefs must be kept from ironizing exaggeration. Swift honors both of these precarious aims throughout much of the last voyage, but he undercuts them in the final chapters of the book. Here, for example, is a passage in which Swift, by confronting us with an overly vivid picture of the Houyhnhnms as *horses*, makes Gulliver's statements about them ironic:

> The *Houyhnhnms* use the hollow Part between the Pastern and the Hoof of their Fore-feet, as we do our Hands, and this with greater Dexterity, than I could at first imagine. I have seen a white Mare of our Family thread a Needle (which I lent her on Purpose) with that Joynt. (4.9.258)

The irony in this passage depends, as it so often does, on exaggerating a statement by making it too literal and too graphic and by taking it to some logical extreme. If Gulliver had simply told us that the Houyhnhnms used their hooves "with greater Dexterity, than I could at first imagine," we could have let his statement pass. When, however, he adds the ludicrously graphic vignette of a horse threading a needle, we read the quoted phrase as an ironic understatement. The politely incredulous phrase "than I could at first imagine" then assumes all its literal force: *no one* could have imagined this feat, precisely because it is impossible. Swift is here beginning to distance himself from Gulliver's astonished admiration of the Houyhnhnms; he is taking us back to our initial expectations about a society of horses, expectations that he has overthrown in the intervening chapters. This is the *ad hominem* part of the ironic devaluation of the ideals presented in part 4.

Immediately after this passage we see Swift begin to state the ideals themselves in an ironic manner that points to his hidden, and indeed ambivalent, dissent. The two major instances of this irony are telling, since both reveal the essentially antihuman features of reason. In the first example, Gulliver explains that the Houyhnhnms' rationality leads them to express "neither Joy nor Grief" at the death of family and friends (4.9.258). Swift then states this ideal ironically by giving an exaggerated and overly vivid example. Gulliver's master was expecting a visit from a friend and his family, but only the wife and children turn up, and that very late:

> she [the friend's wife] made two Excuses, first for her Husband,
> who, as she said, happened that very Morning to *Lhnuwnh*.
> The Word is strongly expressive in their Language, but not eas-
> ily rendered into *English*; it signifies, *to retire to his first Mother*.
> Her Excuse for not coming sooner, was, that her Husband dying
> late in the Morning, she was a good while consulting her Ser-
> vants about a convenient Place where his Body should be laid.
> (4.9.258–59)

As we see in this example, when Swift wants (perhaps unconsciously) to attack the very ideal of reason that he has set up, and
that derives ultimately from the strictures of the superego, he first
states ironically reason's prohibition against mourning. This point
of attack is intriguingly counter to one's expectations, for certainly we would think the attack on reason would come from
another quarter—from the libidinal impulses to which reason
(here almost equivalent to the superego) forbids expression.
Instead, we have the refusal to mourn. Why? When we read the
passage, it seems clear that the underlying psychic identification is
with the dead friend who is being mourned by no one, not by
wife, nor children, nor friends. The reason for this identification
will become clearer if we turn immediately to the second major
example of how Swift states ironically the ideals of reason.

The Houyhnhnms finally decide, in one of their general
assemblies, that Gulliver's master, in accordance with the dictates
of reason, must expel Gulliver from the country. Gulliver
describes his reaction on hearing this news from his master:

> I was struck with the utmost Grief and Despair at my Master's
> Discourse; and being unable to support the Agonies I was under,
> I fell into a Swoon at his Feet: When I came to myself, he told
> me, that he concluded I had been dead. (For these People are
> subject to no such Imbecilities of Nature) I answered, in a faint
> Voice, that Death would have been too great an Happiness; that
> although I could not blame the Assembly's *Exhortation*, or the
> Urgency of his Friends; yet in my weak and corrupt Judgment, I
> thought it might consist with Reason to have been less rigorous.
> (4.10.264)

In this passage we find the culmination of many of the psychic
trends that we have observed in *Gulliver's Travels*. We particularly notice that Gulliver takes the part of the powerful adults yet
again (as he did in Lilliput and especially in Brobdingnag), even

when he thereby sides masochistically against himself. He acquiesces in his own punishment. But we also find here that Gulliver
murmurs, in what I take to be ironic tones, against the adults'
harshness: "yet in my weak and corrupt Judgment, I thought it
might consist with Reason to have been less rigorous." One might
perhaps want to argue that there is no irony here, and yet the
exaggeration, both in Gulliver's self-abasement and in the attenu-
ation of his complaint, is bound to suggest—especially in the context of this work—that irony is present. But whose irony is it? In
one traditional approach, we judge Gulliver to be speaking sin-
cerely, while attributing the irony here to Swift the author. Yet we
drive too absolute a wedge between author and character when
we take this approach. The extent to which Swift identifies with
his character Gulliver, and is present in this character, emerges
much more clearly when we see that Gulliver himself is being
ironic here, though his irony is unconscious. One might expect
that any ambivalence in Swift would be split up so that one side
would remain with the author and the other be attributed to his
character Gulliver, but on the whole Swift cannot really manage
such an easy resolution. Instead, Swift's own ambivalence, though
somewhat transformed, is reflected in splits within the character
of Gulliver. The irony here belongs to the child who knows that,
from the point of view of the adults and the laws of reason they
espouse, his own thinking is "weak and corrupt." And there is
something in the child that truly accepts this judgment of his own
wishful thinking. But there is something else in the child that
rebels and that believes in his own judgment. Indeed, the child
does more than simply *resist* the laws of reason that reality itself,
as well as adult authority, is forcing on him; he also succeeds in
finding contradictions within these laws. This approach of exposing the absurdities—the self-contradictions—within the very precepts that one is mouthing, lies at the very heart of irony. The
child Gulliver rejects the conclusions that are being imposed on
him by adult reason; they appear alien to him not only in the cat-
astrophic results they would bring but even by virtue of their
belonging not to him but to the adult world. Yet even his weak
rebellion is borrowed from the adults: Is your powerful reason, he
asks, not itself inconsistent and therefore unreasonable? "I
thought it might consist with Reason to have been less rigorous."

   As I have suggested, what is so odd about the Gulliver-Swift
revolt against the laws of reason is that it seems motivated more by a

sense of fear and betrayal than by a desire to free the libidinal drives from the bondage of the antihedonistic superego. Indeed, Gulliver complains against reason, not simply because it is separating him from the beloved figures with whom he has identified, but precisely because it is condemning him to live among those who recall him to his own sexuality and aggressiveness. At some level, however, Gulliver must realize that, through his identification with the Houyhnhnms, he has tried to make an inhuman bargain with the superego and the laws of reason and that this bargain can only lead to a terrifying downward spiral of self-destruction that can neither be regretted nor mourned by the implacable agency with which he has cast his lot. Gulliver has identified with—internalized—an ideal against which, being human, he is bound to transgress and whose severe and unyielding punishment he is bound to inflict upon himself. And the more he attempts to escape from his fears, uncertainties, and ambivalences by identifying even more completely with the adult ideals of reason (represented by the Houyhnhnms), the more he condemns himself to masochistic punishment. It is easy enough to see why Gulliver and his creator fear, and murmur against, such ideals—and why Gulliver mourns for himself. It is also easy to see why the rebellion is covert, even unconscious: once a person is caught in this masochistic cycle of self-hatred and self-punishment, the ideals enforced by the superego seem to offer the only chance for an escape. Only a more perfect identification with those ideals, such as Gulliver thinks to achieve in Houyhnhnmland, can carry one away from that sexual and aggressive part of oneself which is hated and must be denied. Once this point in the vicious cycle is reached, the character Gulliver naturally falls apart (in a kind of cautionary tale), and Swift the author—as a way of distancing himself from Gulliver's inescapable predicament—shifts his ironic attack, which is now directed not so much against the ideals themselves as against Gulliver's (and his own) identification with these ideals. The pathos of the Swift/Gulliver rebellion lies precisely in the fact that it can end only in this self-directed, masochistic attack. The other-directed irony, however exuberant it may have seemed, must ultimately be turned on the ironist himself, or his stand-in; and the masochism that tinges all irony reaches full flower here, as if the masochism were somehow more fundamental than the aggression. And yet—crucially, as we will see—Swift the ironist denies this turn by attempting to divide himself once and for all from his stand-in, Gulliver.

The case of *Gulliver's Travels* suggests that the ironist, writing in the ironic mode, cannot give unequivocal consent to any ideal. On the other hand, the reverse is also true: when the ironist repeats the words—the ideals and commands—of authority with the apparent intention of mocking them, the mockery may in fact conceal a measure of acceptance as well. Thus, Gulliver's desperate and fatal attempt to identify with authority undoubtedly represents a similar, if perhaps attenuated, identification on the part of Swift himself. And even at the end of *Gulliver's Travels*, when horses become horses again and Gulliver's praise of them threatens to contaminate all of part 4 with retroactive irony (an irony that has been threatening, and only partly suspended, since the beginning), we still cannot say that the Houyhnhnms' ideal of reason has been definitively rejected—as the work of many "hard-school" critics would remind us. The climax to *Gulliver's Travels* perfectly well illustrates the ambivalent relation to ideals that lies close to the center of all irony.

CHAPTER 3

Kafka's Trial *and the Retreat from Irony*

In the chapter on *Gulliver's Travels*, we looked at the psychological underpinnings of what is perhaps the most classic instance in literature of the extended use of verbal irony. In other words, no one would dispute that what we have in Swift's novel is irony, and, indeed, irony that fits very neatly into the traditional definition that comes to us from rhetoric. If one believes with the lawyers and with such literary critics as M. H. Abrams—and many other critics would certainly dispute this notion—that hard cases make bad law, then it makes much sense for us to concentrate on a central, "classical" instance in our investigation. But there is sense, too, in looking at the marginal, and that is what I propose to do in this chapter. For our investigation of *Gulliver's Travels* has left a major question unanswered. We still do not understand very well why irony should be connected not just with the sadistic tendencies that obviously lie behind it but with masochistic impulses as well. We have certainly seen the connection to masochism not only in Swift but even in the rudimentary paradigms of irony we analyzed in chapter 1, yet we have not fully defined what the connection is. To do so, we need to look at a "hard" case, the case of Franz Kafka's novel *Der Prozess* (*The Trial*).[1]

Kafka is a writer whom we would instinctively label as "ironic." But in this case our label would often be a loose one. Theorists from Friedrich Schlegel to the New Critics have redefined, and broadened, the meaning of the word *irony,* but always in ways that at least some other critics have been unable to subscribe to. Out of this rich tradition we would have no trouble finding concepts that would apply to Kafka and define him as ironic, yet these concepts might not have much to do with the traditional definition of irony, or even with each other. Furthermore, if we examine a book like *The Trial*, we have a surprisingly hard time locating instances, other than relatively isolated ones, of traditional forms of verbal irony. Does this mean that we must give up thinking of *The Trial* as an ironic book so long as we retain the rhetorical definition of irony?

Of course, one might not especially care that Kafka's *Trial* seems poor in verbal irony. But in my view this phenomenon invites investigation for two reasons. First, we would very much like to connect our intuitive sense that Kafka is ironic with the most concrete sense in which it is possible for a critic to use the term *ironic*. And second, Kafka's novel is full of peculiar passages that seem as if they ought to be ironic but, finally, lack a certain quality of tone and shading ordinarily necessary for verbal irony. We want to understand these borderline cases, and if possible the psychology behind them, to see if they can tell us anything more about the psychological underpinnings of verbal irony in literature.

As an example of one of these passages, let us look at the famous opening sentence of *The Trial*: "Jemand mußte Josef K. verleumdet haben, denn ohne daß er etwas Böses getan hätte, wurde er eines Morgens verhaftet" [Someone must have been telling lies about Joseph K., for without having done anything wrong he was arrested one fine morning].[2] When a reader first encounters this sentence, he is bound to take it more or less as the opinion of the author, and he is bound to read it straight—that is, the author is not being ironic, pulling the reader's leg, or lying to the reader. Sooner or later, however, any attentive reader of *The Trial* will realize that Kafka does *not* consider his hero as having done nothing wrong, and he certainly does not consider his hero as innocent. There is even external evidence for this assertion, since Kafka, in his notebooks, refers to Josef K. as "der Schuldige" [the guilty one].[3] But there is no real hint in the opening sentence that the author does not share the opinion that seems to be coming directly from him. Indeed, it must be said that the hints elsewhere in the book are subtle enough that not a few readers have missed them and have concluded that Josef K. is innocent. How, then, are we to take the opening sentence? If we hew to the traditional rhetorical definition of irony, we certainly cannot consider the sentence ironic. A speaker may hide his irony from some members of his audience, as indeed Socrates did, but if he hides it from his entire audience, if he does not betray his true opinion by some oddity of diction or gesture, then the speaker is doing something other than speaking ironically. Ordinarily, in fact, we would simply say that the speaker is lying. But Kafka does not seem to be lying either.

Since we are dealing with a work of literature, there is one readily available alternative to the two possibilities just mentioned, to the possibilities that the author is speaking ironically or that he is lying. The author, namely, might be speaking "fictionally." Such a formulation, in itself, does not really mean very much, but the New Critics gave it a clear and pedagogically useful sense that remains with us today. We learned from them to consider the possibility (or even to make the methodological assumption) that the author is not speaking in his own voice but rather is pretending to be some fictional character, more or less fully presented. But in the case of Kafka's *Trial* this expedient seems less viable than it ordinarily does. The speaking voice is too neutral, too transparent, to all appearances too disinterested for us to let it congeal into a character or even a half-character. Yet the reader also realizes, eventually, that the narrative voice scarcely strays from the consciousness of the main character, Josef K. So Kafka's voice in the novel is fictionalized in the sense that it reflects the thoughts of a fictional character. But this character exists in the novel in his own right, apart from the speaking voice, and we need to understand why the character Josef K. should be doubled in this fashion, appearing once *in propria persona* and once in the voice of what formally appears to be an omniscient narrator. Something is backwards here. Why should the authoritative speaking voice be infected with the thoughts of the main character, a limited and deluded figure? The answer seems far from obvious.

A theoretical reflection is in order here. From a strictly literary point of view, that is, from a formalist point of view, an explanation of "fictionality" might be a sufficiently explanatory final term. From a psychological or psychoanalytic point of view, however, we cannot stop with this term. One needs to ask why this author, or any author, speaks with a fictional voice—and a fictional voice, moreover, of a specific kind. In the preceding paragraph I referred to the most sophisticated formalist procedure for analyzing a case where the author is saying something that he believes to be untrue but is neither lying nor speaking ironically. I have suggested that this procedure will not work very well for the kind of disingenuous statements that we find in Kafka's *Trial*. To say that Kafka is speaking in a fictionalized voice does not begin

to answer the most interesting questions raised by Kafka's authorial stance in the novel. Nor does such an explanation provide an
adequate third possibility—besides lying or irony—for analyzing
a sentence like the one we are looking at.

So far, we have said that this sentence shows similarity to verbal irony in that the author does not himself believe his own statement to be true; indeed, Kafka might be said to believe the *opposite*
of the statement he utters. We can be more specific about this similarity to verbal irony. For the opening sentence is only the first line
in a litany of protestations that recur throughout the novel pro-
claiming K.'s innocence. When K. fails to stop the beating that is
being inflicted on the warder Franz, "es war nicht seine Schuld"
(114) [it was not his (K.'s) fault (88)]. Or even in absolute terms, as
we read in a later chapter, "Es gab keine Schuld" (168) [There was
no such guilt (127)]. The litany culminates during K.'s visit to the
painter Titorelli, where the expressions of innocence are put
directly into the mouths of K. and his interlocutor. "'Sind Sie
unschuldig?' fragte er [i.e., Titorelli]. 'Ja,' sagte K." (200) ["Are
you innocent?" he (Titorelli) asked. "Yes," said K. (149)]. Then K.
adds: "Ich bin vollständig unschuldig" [I am completely innocent].
The painter almost immediately repeats his question, and from
that point on, he continues to allude to K.'s innocence by formally
assuming the truth of K.'s claim. Three times in succession he uses
phrases like "da Sie vollständig unschuldig sind" (205) [as you are
completely innocent (152)]. K. reacts to these phrases:

> Die wiederholte Erwähnung seiner Unschuld wurde K. schon
> lästig. Ihm schien es manchmal als mache der Maler durch
> solche Bemerkungen einen günstigen Ausgang des Processes zur
> Voraussetzung seiner Hilfe, die dadurch natürlich in sich selbst
> zusammenfiel. (205)
>
> [The repeated mention of his innocence was already making
> K. impatient. At moments it seemed to him as if the painter
> were offering his help on the assumption that the trial would
> turn out well, which made his offer worthless. (152)]

As usual, K. misunderstands the source of his anxiety. The
second sentence here is built on a complicated logical puzzle that
goes something like this: K. and Titorelli both share the unspoken
assumption that if K. seeks help, then *ipso facto* he is guilty; if he
were innocent he wouldn't need any help. K., of course, is trying
to avoid acknowledging this assumption, and Titorelli is ostensi-

bly cooperating with K. in this avoidance. Titorelli both accepts K.'s claim of innocence and discusses with K. ways in which he might help K. in his trial. But the two sides of this "and" are mutually contradictory, so that the more often the painter puts the two things together as if they were logically compatible, the more he is forcing K. to confront their mutual incompatibility. K. is irritated with the painter because he thinks the painter is being illogical, but at a deeper level K.'s irritation stems from the fact that Titorelli is exposing the illogicality of K.'s own position. Titorelli is merely taking what K. says and repeating it back to K.—several times and in logically uncomfortable contexts.

Titorelli does not seem to be speaking with conscious irony. That is, he does not seem to be aware of the way he is exposing the absurdity of K.'s position merely by repeating back to K., with a certain emphasis, exactly what K. has been saying to him. But there is no question that the structure of Titorelli's remarks reminds us of rhetorical irony, reminds us in fact of one of the most famous examples of irony in literature, Mark Antony's funeral oration over the corpse of Caesar. Consider an excerpt from that speech:

> He [Caesar] was my friend, faithful and just to me;
> But Brutus says he was ambitious,
> And Brutus is an honourable man.
> He hath brought many captives home to Rome,
> Whose ransoms did the general coffers fill:
> Did this in Caesar seem ambitious?
> When that the poor have cried, Caesar hath wept;
> Ambition should be made of sterner stuff:
> Yet Brutus says he was ambitious,
> And Brutus is an honourable man.
> You all did see that on the Lupercal
> I thrice presented him a kingly crown,
> Which he did thrice refuse. Was this ambition?
> Yet Brutus says he was ambitious,
> And sure he is an honourable man.
> I speak not to disprove what Brutus spoke,
> But here I am to speak what I do know.[4]

The refrain in Mark Antony's speech is paralleled by Titorelli's repeated references to K.'s innocence. Moreover, Mark Antony is engaged in the classical move alloted to rhetorical irony—to blame through praise—and this move might also be seen to characterize Titorelli's remarks, though we do not find in them Mark Antony's obviously conscious intention. Finally, both speeches present (formally) unanalyzed logical contradictions. No auditor could accept these contradictions without further interpretation, which would probably involve disputing one of the contradictory assertions. Nevertheless, the speaker in both cases presents these assertions as if they could all be simultaneously valid. Mark Antony, of course, does not mean for his auditors to accept their simultaneous validity; he is being disingenuous in saying, "I speak not to disprove what Brutus spoke." But with Titorelli, we have no clear indication that he himself sees the absurdity of what he is repeating, and K. seems to have no more than a glimmer of this absurdity.

Is *anyone* being ironic here? Everything we have just said about Titorelli's remarks points to an almost classical structure of verbal (rhetorical) irony. Moreover, we have previously noted that irony, at its psychological origin, often involves repeating back to the powerful adult something that the adult herself has said, while at the same time subtly exposing the absurdity of the adult's pronouncements. This kind of repeating back certainly seems to be present in Titorelli's remarks. But if the irony does not belong to Titorelli, then it can only belong to Kafka himself. So we test the proposition that Kafka is being ironic at K.'s expense, that Kafka, by stating with irony and through his mouthpiece Titorelli that K. is innocent, means to convey his belief that K. is guilty. We might then want to reread all the other remarks about K.'s innocence, often coming directly from the authorial voice, as being in some sense ironic, even though we did not originally take them as such.

This solution does not work very well if we trust our natural reactions to the Titorelli scene. For if Titorelli is not aware of the absurdity of his remarks, then the remarks boomerang back onto the painter; *he* rather than K. tends to become their target. The ostensible ironist becomes the butt of the irony. Thus when Titorelli says that he can be of great help to K., here for once the reader senses that Kafka is being ironic. Kafka means for us to conclude the opposite of what we hear Titorelli saying; the painter will obviously be of no help at all. It is as if, as a result of Mark Antony's speech, Shakespeare directed attention away from Brutus and instead called into question Mark Antony's own ability to think logically, given the non sequiturs he utters in his speech. As so often in Kafka's novel, we are drawn back to K.'s viewpoint whenever we seem to be escaping to a more objective, or at least different, mentality. Thus, even in the Titorelli scene the potential irony at K.'s expense seems to be defused. Here, as elsewhere in the book, we may conclude through analysis that Kafka thinks his hero is guilty, but we cannot quite catch Kafka saying so; we can't really take the affirmations of K.'s innocence as being obviously ironic.

The conclusion we must draw is that Kafka sets up a potentially ironic way of speaking about his hero but then veers away from the irony or at least defuses it where it is not altogether avoided. We can understand well enough why an author might not want to be ironic about his hero. For example, the author might identify so closely with his hero that he could not suffer the hero, and thus himself, to come under this kind of attack. And certainly any reader senses a strong identification between K. and his author; even the initial that is all we learn of the hero's surname says much in this regard. But with *The Trial* we have a considerably harder question. For we need to ask why Kafka would skirt so close to an ironic treatment of his hero and at the same time draw back repeatedly from the irony he seems to introduce. To answer this question, we will have to examine more closely the complex role irony plays within the psyche. For it is not only a *defense* of the ego, the descendant of the child's casuistical weapon against the over-powerful adults, but also a weapon that is often turned against the ego itself. The relation between these two functions is yet another manifestation of the psychic ambivalence that lies so close to the nature of irony. This relation also begins to explain the sadomasochistic tinge that we have repeatedly found in the instances of verbal irony that we have examined.

KAFKA'S "LETTER TO HIS FATHER"

To get at the peculiar quality of the near-irony in Kafka's *Trial*, we should first examine several clues Kafka gives us in the "Brief an den Vater" ("Letter to His Father"). There are three strains to notice here. First is the series of remarks about the *father's* innocence—for example:

> Diese Deine übliche Darstellung halte ich nur soweit für richtig,
> daß auch ich glaube, Du seist gänzlich schuldlos an unserer Ent-
> fremdung. Aber ebenso gänzlich schuldlos bin auch ich.
>
> [This, your usual way of representing it (i.e., the estrange-
> ment between father and son), I regard as accurate only in so far
> as I too believe you are entirely blameless in the matter of our
> estrangement. But I am equally entirely blameless.][5]

A double anxiety lies behind this passage: Kafka cannot bear to
accuse his father of guilt, yet on the other hand he fears that either
one or the other of them must be guilty. He is desperately trying
to reassure himself that they can both be innocent, but this reassurance (like all reassurance) is a rationalization that attempts to
cover over a more deeply rooted, and contrary, belief. Consequently, Kafka cannot absolve his father of guilt without at the
same time convicting himself—a result that he wishes most
heartily to avoid. In the present passage, Kafka extricates himself
from the difficulty by means of unconvincing denials all around.

The problem with this solution is that it is too neutral. If the
denials are not accepted (and they cannot be), then *either* of the
two mutually exclusive propositions can be overturned—either
the son is guilty or the father is guilty; for Kafka, here, does not
prejudice the case of which of the two propositions is false. But let
us look at a second passage:

> Jedenfalls waren wir so verschieden und in dieser Verschieden-
> heit einander so gefährlich, daß, wenn man es hätte etwa im
> voraus ausrechnen wollen, wie ich, das langsam sich entwik-
> kelnde Kind, und Du, der fertige Mann, sich zu einander verhal-
> ten werden, man hätte annehmen können, daß Du mich einfach
> niederstampfen wirst, daß nichts von mir übrigbleibt. Das ist
> nun nicht geschehn, das Lebendige läßt sich nicht ausrechnen,
> aber vielleicht ist Ärgeres geschehn. Wobei ich Dich aber immer-
> fort bitte, nicht zu vergessen, daß ich niemals im entferntesten
> an eine Schuld Deinerseits glaube. (147)
>
> [However it was, we were so different and in our difference
> so dangerous to each other that, if anyone had tried to calculate
> in advance how I, the slowly developing child, and you, the full-
> grown man, would stand to each other, he could have assumed
> that you would simply trample me underfoot so that nothing
> was left of me. Well, that didn't happen. Nothing alive can be
> calculated. But perhaps something worse happened. And in say-

ing this I would all the time beg of you not to forget that I never, and not even for a single moment, believe any guilt to be on your side. (141)]

If one compares the two passages, one notices a significant difference in the underlying logical structures. The first passage says "not A, but also not B," while implying that either A or B—one or the other—must be true. The second passage leads us through enthymemic reasoning (i.e., syllogisms with the major premise implied but not stated); then, when it reaches the necessary conclusion (that you, the father, are guilty), it not only refuses the conclusion but asserts in the strongest possible terms the opposite of the expected conclusion. Both passages, in other words, exhibit logical contradictions, but only the second forces this contradiction so blatantly on the reader that neither he, nor presumably the author, can ignore it. In the first passage we see the author burying his head in the sand; in the second, we hear the voice of irony—the author means the opposite of what he is saying, and saying in an exaggerated fashion.

We see, then, a kind of progression in these two passages. Kafka is pressing toward a dangerous accusation of his father. In the first passage, the breath of accusation is faint; in the second, it is much stronger. In the first passage, Kafka only suggests retroactively that the father is guilty (if not B, then perhaps A after all). In the second, he draws back from an aggressive accusation only with a last-minute ironic denial. Kafka has to attack his father; this seems to be his deepest need (and the proposition that "either you or I must be guilty" seems more a result than a cause of this need). The defensive cover of irony seems to allow him his boldest attacks.

But this account, according to which the irony in the second passage would show the most typical psychological motivations we have associated with irony, needs some modification. For oddly enough, the second passage, which seems to end so ironically when read in isolation, appears much less ironic when put back in the context of the "Letter to His Father." However great Kafka's need is to attack his father, his fear of doing so marginally outweighs it. The more obvious the attack, the more desperately Kafka must disavow it. The desperation, in fact, passes for a form of sincerity, so that Kafka's repeated insistences that his father is

innocent do not finally strike us in the same way as Mark
Anthony's assurances about Brutus. On the other hand, Kafka's
exquisite self-consciousness and literary sensitivity do not allow
us to interpret his irony as unconscious. The irony is there, but the
terrible fear with which it is mingled robs it of its customary
effect. We remember that the addressee of the letter—and, in a
way, of all Kafka's writings—is the father himself: "Mein
Schreiben handelte von Dir, ich klagte dort ja nur, was ich an
Deiner Brust nicht klagen konnte" (192) [My writing was all
about you; all I did there, after all, was to bemoan what I could
not bemoan upon your breast (177)]. This addressee *must* believe
in the denial with which Kafka couples his ironic attack. Kafka
works to make the denial convincing.[6]

If we turn now to a second strain in the "Letter to His
Father," we will see yet another reason why Kafka's irony shows a
different quality from ordinary verbal irony, even as it derives
from the usual roots of such irony. Here Kafka describes the origins of his irony:

> Um mich Dir gegenüber nur ein wenig zu behaupten, zum Teil
> auch aus einer Art Rache fing ich bald an kleine Lächer-
> lichkeiten, die ich an Dir bemerkte, zu beobachten, zu sammeln,
> zu übertreiben . . . Solcher verschiedener Beobachtungen gab es
> natürlich eine Menge; ich war glücklich über sie, es gab für mich
> Anlaß zu Getuschel und Spaß, Du bemerktest es manchmal, är-
> gertest Dich darüber, hieltest es für Bosheit, Respecktlosigkeit,
> aber glaube mir, es war nichts anderes für mich, als ein übrigens
> untaugliches Mittel zur Selbsterhaltung, es waren Scherze, wie
> man sie über Götter und Könige verbreitet, Scherze, die mit dem
> tiefsten Respekt nicht nur sich verbinden lassen, sondern sogar
> zu ihm gehören. (166–67)
>
> [In order to assert myself a very little in relation to you, and
> partly too from a kind of vengefulness, I soon began to observe
> little ridiculous things about you, collecting them and exagger-
> ating them . . . There were, of course, plenty of such observa-
> tions. I was happy about them; they were for me an occasion for
> whispering and joking; you sometimes noticed it and were
> angry about it, taking it to be malice and lack of respect for you,
> but believe me it was for me nothing other than a means—
> moreover, a useless one—of attempted self-preservation; they
> were jokes of the kind that is made everywhere about gods and
> kings, jokes that are not only compatible with the profoundest
> respect but which are indeed part and parcel of it. (156)]

The passage does not speak precisely of irony, but the process it describes is the very essence of irony: finding something ridiculous in a powerful figure and exposing the absurdity by representing it in an exaggerated form. Kafka's claim that such joking was only a part of his respect is unconvincing, but it does make clear that the powerless child resorted to this kind of indirection as his only means of revenge.

The question remains, however, as to what constituted the father's "kleine Lächerlichkeiten" [small absurdities]. The proper answer, I think, is logical contradiction. Certainly in *The Trial* one of Kafka's insistent, worrying themes is the logical contradiction into which the authorities fall—and even the logical contradictions of the world order itself. In fact, logic itself is one of the major motifs in the novel. But logical contradiction is a concern not only of Kafka; throughout the present essay, we have time and again found logical contradiction to be at the very heart of irony. We have found this to be true not only in our analyses of verbal ironies in everyday speech and in literature but also in the obsessive symptoms that show an ironic structure. Paradigmatic here is Reik's case of the nobleman who thought of all servants as devils. When we attack the powerful with our ironies, we are accusing them, in part, of logical self-contradiction. This is a harsh stricture we place on our parents, conformity to the unyielding dictates of logic, but Kafka makes clear why we impose this standard:

> Für mich als Kind war aber alles, was Du mir zuriefst, geradezu Himmelsgebot, ich vergaß es nie, es blieb mir das wichtigste Mittel zur Beurteilung der Welt, vor allem zur Beurteilung Deiner selbst und da versagtest Du vollständig. (155)
>
> [But for me as a child everything you shouted at me was positively a heavenly commandment, I never forgot it, it remained for me the most important means of forming a judgment of the world, above all of forming a judgment of you yourself, and there you failed entirely. (147)]

And yet—when in *The Trial* Kafka exposes the absurdities of the authorities, the irony we might expect does not quite emerge. This is true even where Kafka writes patches of indirect discourse, which as we have seen furnishes the most natural home for irony. (The speaker purports to be giving the words of another, but the very fact that he puts them in his own mouth introduces a new perspective on them and opens the way for slight, but malevolent, rewordings.) At the beginning of chapter 7, "Advokat-Fabrikant-Maler" [Lawyer-Manufacturer-Painter], we hear a kind of double indirect discourse: we get K.'s thoughts through free indirect discourse, and among these thoughts is a review of what Huld, the lawyer, typically says to K. during K.'s visits to him. The lawyer's remarks themselves are represented as a lengthy speech in indirect discourse. At first the indirect discourse in this speech is marked by the special subjunctive verb forms German uses for that mode, but afterwards Kafka switches freely back and forth between this subjunctive and the ordinary indicative. Here is an excerpt, regarding the "first plea" that the lawyer is still preparing for submission to the court on K.'s behalf. The lawyer has explained that although the first plea is vitally important (since the first impression the court receives may well determine the future course of the trial), rumor has it that this first plea is often lost or simply not read:

> Das alles sei bedauerlich, aber nicht ganz ohne Berechtigung, K. möge doch nicht außer acht lassen, daß das Verfahren nicht öffentlich sei, es kann, wenn das Gericht es für nötig hält, öffentlich werden, das Gesetz aber schreibt Öffentlichkeit nicht vor. Infolgedessen sind auch die Schriften des Gerichtes, vor allem die Anklageschrift dem Angeklagten und seiner Verteidigung unzugänglich, man weiß daher im allgemeinen nicht oder wenigstens nicht genau, wogegen sich die erste Eingabe zu richten hat, sie kann daher eigentlich nur zufälligerweise etwas enthalten, was für die Sache von Bedeutung ist. (151–52)
>
> [It was all very regrettable, but not wholly without justification. K. must remember that the proceedings were not public; they could certainly, if the Court considered it necessary, become public, but the Law did not prescribe that they must be made public. Naturally, therefore, the legal records of the case, and above all the actual charge-sheets, were inaccessible to the accused and his counsel, consequently one did not know in general, or at least did not know with any precision, what charges to meet in the first plea; accordingly it could only be by pure chance that it contained really relevant matter. (115)]

The incipient verbal irony in this passage is evident: The court's shabby tendency to neglect the first petition is, the lawyer says, "not wholly without justification," but the justification offered rests on apparently absurd premises that lead to apparently absurd conclusions. The author of the book must actually believe something like the opposite of the first sentence quoted above. The Muirs' translation, incorrectly, emphasizes the irony. In using the word *naturally*, the Muirs imply a standard of ordinary common sense, and such a standard is grossly violated by the court's behavior; the author could not possibly share the judgment implied by "naturally." Kafka's German, however, actually uses the word *infolgedessen* [as a result of which]—a more neutrally descriptive word that emphasizes the court's adherence to its own logic. The point here is that the Muirs understandably pick up on the potential irony in this passage, while Kafka himself refuses to extend the irony. We can go further, to say that Kafka actually damps down the irony. How does he do this?

When Reik's patient, the young nobleman, unconsciously exposes the illogic of his parents' teaching—by producing a system that ironically makes their teaching consistent again—he is mounting a covert attack against them. He "expects" this attack to succeed because the parents (probably, in fact, dead) would accept as binding on themselves the ethical requirement of logical consistency. Swift offers a similar case. If he exposes through irony, with its self-defended aggressiveness, the ethical failings and inconsistencies of authority, then he has successfully attacked this authority. Kafka, however, does not expect his irony to be efficacious in this way. In the present passage Kafka's irony screams out that the policy of the court is totally unjustified. But the court has its own logic—or, more precisely, its own premises; and the court's logic wins, because it is based on the power of the court and of authority generally. Against such an opponent, irony is not really a weapon: irony is not quite itself if its target does not admit the ethical justice of consistency or if the target is indifferent to having its inconsistency exposed. And for Kafka, authority is of this diabolical sort, as we see in the "Letter to His Father":

> Deine Meinung war richtig, jede andere war verrückt, überspannt, meschugge, nicht normal. Dabei war Dein Selbstvertrauen so groß, daß Du gar nicht konsequent sein mußtest und doch nicht aufhörtest Recht zu haben . . . Du bekamst für mich das Rätselhafte, das alle Tyrannen haben, deren Recht auf ihrer Person, nicht auf dem Denken begründet ist. (152)
>
> [Your opinion was correct, every other was mad, wild, *meschugge*, not normal. With all this your self-confidence was so great that you had no need to be consistent at all and yet never ceased to be in the right . . . For me you took on the enigmatic

quality that all tyrants have whose rights are based on their person and not on reason. (145)]

So even if Kafka's irony proceeds from the normal psychological roots, his lack of faith in irony as a weapon against authority deprives Kafka's irony of overtones we normally pick up in verbal irony. But by looking a little more closely at the passage we have been analyzing, we should be able to see a deeper reason why the overtones of Kafka's quasi-ironic statements are so unusual. We have said, and this is one of the major hypotheses of a psychoanalytic approach to irony, that a person means what she says and that when a statement has several different levels of meaning, some of them perhaps appearing to contradict one another, she still means all of them simultaneously. Consider again the sentence: "Das alles sei bedauerlich, aber nicht ganz ohne Berechtigung" [It was all very regrettable, but not wholly without justification]. As we have said, the author of this sentence is being ironic, in that at some level he believes the situation to be, in fact, "wholly without justification." But on the other hand, Kafka allows the lawyer to deliver a lengthy justification of the court's procedure, one that shows a great deal of internal consistency. We might note, too, that in German the word *Berechtigung,* here translated as "justification," also has the sense of "warrant" or "authority." Hence, the sentence reminds us that the court's warrant for acting as it does might derive from its *power* rather than from any ethically and logically valid account of its procedure. In other words, as we read the quoted sentence in its context, the ironic overtones of the sentence tend to fade away. We are willing to accept the unpleasant notion that the court is acting "nicht ganz ohne Berechtigung."

The loss of these ironic overtones reflects, I believe, a crucial psychological process going on within the author of the novel. Any ironist is speaking with two voices: his own and that of the authorities of childhood. In ordinary verbal irony, we don't have much trouble placing these voices at different "depths" within the psyche. The voice of authority is adopted as a defense. Even when it is adopted unconsciously, so that the speaker is not *aware* that he is merely repeating (though with a difference) the words of authority, an observer is able to discern that this is not the most authentic voice of the speaker. The speaker's rage and aggression against authority are in fact more central to him—to whatever self lies deepest within him. But this is the stratification that Kafka comes so close to obscuring. To be sure, Kafka's novel is, in some sense, a long indictment of the tyrannies of authority (and the superego), but on the whole the victim is Josef K., the stand-in for Kafka's "self" (as we have just been using the term). The authorities turn out to be right, and Kafka believes that they *are* right and are indeed acting with complete justification. No matter how deeply we look, we have trouble locating any kind of consistently available self who is striking back against the inhuman demands of authority and superego. We simply cannot locate the voice that we so easily hear behind the façade of verbal irony. As we will now see, the crux of the problem here lies in the differing forms of psychological identification into which Kafka and the ordinary verbal ironist enter.

Before taking up the problem of identification, however, it may be well to admit that as we study this marginal case of irony, our discussion of Kafka and *The Trial* is bound to be more suggestive of psychoanalytic diagnosis than was our account of Swift and *Gulliver's Travels*. Verbal irony is itself a somewhat unsatisfactory solution to problems of defense and aggression—essentially a neurotic one in cases where it is habitual and compulsive—so the failure, or unwillingness, to follow through with an incipient irony would seem to indicate a speaker whose ability to defend himself and make aggressive contact with the world is especially fragile. Indeed, the very singularity of Kafka's irony suggests that there is a *need* for diagnosis here, if we are to come to a better understanding of the psychological underpinnings of irony. Kafka himself was, of course, the first practitioner of the kind of Kafka analysis we are doing here; he was hardly averse to the most extravagant assertions about the symptoms produced by his psychological conflicts—repeatedly claiming, for example, that his tuberculosis was a disease that had begun in his head, not his lungs.[7] So if we regard Kafka's brand of irony, whether it appears in a novel like *The Trial* or in a piece of autobiographical writing like the "Letter to His Father," as a reflection—a symptom—of his psychological makeup, then we are following a lead offered by Kafka himself.

The terms *symptom* and *diagnosis* are, of course, somewhat misleading, in that they suggest short labels that solve the puzzle and end discussion; indeed, they are often used to dismiss psychoanalytic criticism as reductive. But in its best forms, psychoanalysis has always respected the depth and mystery of what is individual (though it does not consider the individual to be *ineffabile*), and its essence has always lain more in exploration than in labelling.[8] In any event, Kafka's works are in no danger of being exhausted or exterminated by any one approach, however successful or unsuccessful it may be in illuminating the texts.

IDENTIFICATION AND IRONY

Since the publication of Anna Freud's *The Ego and the Mechanisms of Defense*, psychoanalysts have generally accepted "identification with the aggressor" as one of the common defenses the ego tends to erect in childhood. The powerful adult threatens or accuses the child, and the child seeks to escape this excruciating inferior position by imagining himself to be this very adult, the aggressor. The child identifies himself, in fantasy, with the adult, but this fantasized identification must rest on some tangible signs of identity. An everyday example would be the child who is scolded by his mother and later turns around and scolds the family dog for the same shortcoming. Here the child's imitation of the mother's strictures and verbal punishment results from—and serves as a symbol of—the child's identification with the mother. Naturally enough, such identification with the aggressor also contributes toward the development of the child's superego, as well as serving as an ego defense. Another example, this one cited by Anna Freud, shows the relevance of this kind of identification to our discussion of verbal irony.

Anna Freud reports the case of an elementary school boy seen in consultation by the psychologist August Aichhorn:

> The [boy's school] master complained that the boy's behavior, when he was blamed or reproved, was quite abnormal. On such occasions he made faces which caused the whole class to burst out laughing. The master's view was that either the boy was consciously making fun of him or else the twitching of his face must be due to some kind of tic. His report was at once corroborated, for the boy began to make faces during the consultation, but, when master, pupil, and psychologist were together, the situation was explained. Observing the two attentively, Aichhorn saw that the boy's grimaces were simply a caricature of the angry expression of the teacher and that, when he had to face a

scolding by the latter, he tried to master his anxiety by involuntarily imitating him. The boy identified himself with the teacher's anger and copied his expression as he spoke, though the imitation was not recognized. Through his grimaces he was assimilating himself to or identifying himself with the dreaded external object.[9]

Though the present case turns on facial expressions rather than words, we can readily see the similarity here between the boy's behavior and the behavior associated with instances of verbal irony as we have analyzed them. Thus, the boy repeats the gestures of the authority (just as in verbal irony the words of the authority are repeated). But in addition, again as in verbal irony, the repetition leaves the authority looking ridiculous; when the teacher's expression is detached from the source of authority that alone makes it fearful, the expression, evaluated "in itself" and on the inappropriate face of a powerless child, is revealed as absurd. Let us accept Aichhorn's testimony that the child was not consciously trying to imitate the teacher, much less ridicule him. Further, let us accept Aichhorn's and Anna Freud's interpretation that the child *was* imitating the teacher unconsciously (as a way of identifying himself with the authority). It does not, however, seem plausible to deny—as Aichhorn and Anna Freud do—that the boy was *also* ridiculing the teacher, just as the teacher suspected. The ridicule, like the imitation, was undoubtedly unconscious, but surely both were in some way intended (in the same way that we have said verbal irony may be unconscious). What we would then find in this example is a most curious constellation: both identification with the aggressor-authority and an attack on this same aggressor-authority. We should note further the masochistic tinge in this attack. Leaving aside the theoretical point that the boy is attacking a figure with whom he is simultaneously identifying, the masochism is evident at an even more "realistic" level: The boy has made his attack in such an obvious way that the teacher cannot fail to react and retaliate. He leaves himself defended only by refusing to allow into consciousness the knowledge of what he is doing; he can therefore always claim that he "didn't mean to" ridicule the teacher. (Notice that this defense is similar to the one theoretically available in irony: the ironist can deny that he "really meant" what his irony implies, and the literal sense of what he has said will support his denial.) In the event, the teacher does retaliate and the boy gets in trouble; the boy's ultimate exoneration—thanks to a visiting psychiatrist—was perhaps the most unforeseeable outcome of all, and should not obscure the self-destructiveness in the boy's behavior.

By expanding on Anna Freud's interpretation of this case, we have made the boy's behavior more difficult to understand, but if we can nonetheless make some sense of its contradictions, we will advance our understanding of verbal irony. In part, the question that needs to be considered is how the boy can both identify with and attack the teacher at the same time. An answer to this question must begin with the observation that no identification is ever total, since, as Harold P. Blum puts it, "no one is totally assimilated or transformed in the process."[10] Indeed, if we are really speaking of identification, this observation is in the nature of a truism, for as other psychoanalysts have pointed out, to "identify" means to identify oneself with someone else; hence, the process of identification takes place only on the basis of an underlying sense of separateness between the self and the other person. An identification, in other words, is an attempt to cover over or bridge a difference. In traditional psychoanalysis, it tends to be conceived of as a process of "introjection": somehow taking into the psyche (and perhaps "incorporating" there) some aspect of the other. But a perhaps more helpful definition is the kind offered recently by S. M. Abend and M. S. Porder: "identifications should be thought of as expressions of unconscious fantasies having in common the idea of being someone else, or of becoming like someone else as a way of achieving the various motives involved in each case."[11] What becomes crucial are the *signs* that are found, erected, or imagined to support this underlying fantasy. But it is easy to see that neither the fantasy nor the symbols of the identification can do away with the underlying difference and that the underlying difference can be the source of a highly ambivalent attitude toward the other person. If, indeed, the identification arises as a defense mechanism to alleviate anxiety, to assuage the fear of being attacked by the powerful adult, then the identification must certainly conceal a—perhaps unconscious—hostility. The questions really are these: What is the *balance* between the identification and the hostility? Which one is concealed by the other? To what extent does either remain unconscious? And, of course, the answer to these questions will vary from case to case. In ordinary verbal irony, however, we tend to see one particular balance, one particular type of relationship between identification and hostility. Here it is the identification that tends to be unconscious, whereas the hostility, the wish to attack, is often quite obvious. When the ironist adopts the words of the authority, he is in some sense defending himself against counterattack ("I've only repeated what you said"), but in another sense he is revealing his identification with the very authority he is attacking (the repetition is a sign of identification)—although, to be sure, this identification itself may be essentially defensive in purpose. We see again that the literal level of an ironic statement is not unmotivated, not simply a veil to be seen through. It reveals, instead, a crucial element in the psychological structure of irony, and, indeed, without the identification this surface level reveals, there could be no ironic statement. We are back to Anna Freud's case: the boy's hostile ridicule is evident enough; what psychoanalysis reveals is the simultaneous existence of his identification with the teacher.

For future reference, let us explore one more aspect of the case. How, that is, do we account for its apparently masochistic result? When, a few years ago, Anna Freud discussed her earlier writings on "identification with the aggressor," she emphasized the tendency in children at play to *reverse* and to *exchange* the roles they have assumed.[12] In the case we are analyzing, this reversal does in fact take place—that is to say, the teacher feels himself attacked—but the further (clearly foreseeable) repercussions to the boy must also belong to the boy's unconscious intentions. The boy connives at his own punishment. Two sorts of psychoanalytic explanation are possible. The first would emphasize the confusing incompleteness of identification. Thus, although the child may identify with the aggressor (and this, we have seen, is the fantasy), he cannot thereby cancel his own identity as the victim. As a result, even as he imagines himself to be the powerful adult aggressor, he still affirms his own sense of who he is by simultaneously making himself the ultimate victim of his own aggression. The second type of explanation would view the boy's ultimate punishment as defensive or exculpatory. The boy's own superego demands that he be punished for his attack on a parent, and it does so in such a way that the boy cannot even embark on his aggression without simultaneously ensuring that he will not go unpunished; the punishment becomes, as it were, a prerequisite for the aggression, so that the boy atones for the crime in order to commit it and in the very act of committing it. One might also say that the boy controls the type of punishment he will receive and thereby forestalls the powerful adult from imposing the severer ones of castration and death, the revenge that the boy actually fears the father figure may exact. As in Anna Freud's example, so with verbal irony in general: as I have tried to show, irony always reveals a more or less pronounced masochistic result, destructive in some way to the ironist herself. The explanations proposed here for the schoolboy's behavior are the kinds of explanation one needs in order to begin untangling the motives for the masochism in verbal irony.

All of what we have said about identification up to this point applies to behavior within the realm of the normal or the neurotic. Psychoanalysts, however, have also spoken of pathological identification, which differs in crucial ways from the conceptual model we have been drawing. As we have said, the more ordinary forms of identification presuppose that the individual has some reasonably secure—if unconscious—sense of the very self that is being identified with some other person. In fact, we use the word *identification* because it seems to presuppose two entities that are being made "identical" to one another. However, the person without this minimal sense of self—such a lack would be characteristic of psychosis or a prepsychotic condition—cannot enter into identifications of this kind. For example, in his "Identification and Its Vicissitudes as Observed in Psychosis," Otto Kernberg, a psychoanalyst, makes these observations about his psychotic patient Miss A.: "It became evident that Miss A. could not separate her own thinking from mine"; further, "the patient was afraid of invasion of her mind by my thoughts and wishes."[13] We are talking now about an identification process that no longer brings things together but, rather, replaces one with the other—as if the self, or ego, could be obliterated thereby. The individual makes the same kinds of identification as does a healthier person, but he has no defense, so to speak, against these identifications. Another psychoanalyst, Jorge E. García Badaracco, speaks in these terms:

> It is my understanding that a *pathological identification* will be the one which incorporates into the psychic apparatus elements of an invasive and demanding nature whose presence will force the other mental functions to restructure and submit to them . . . [Pathological identifications] seem to be bonds that stifle spontaneity and generate submission and paralysis through introjection and introjective identification. This seems

to be caused by total invasion or intrusion into a fragile and immature ego which, in order to survive, is forced to transform itself into the other, to be the other, losing what may be its own true apects. These identifications are alienating since the ego has been displaced by a strange and intrusive object that has possessed it as if "demonically."[14]

If we are right in saying that unconscious (or even conscious) identification with the powerful adult always makes up one of the strata of verbal irony, then we must be speaking of the healthier kinds of identification. Clearly, pathological identification, as we have spoken of it here, could not coexist with irony. For irony requires that the ego have enough sense of its own separateness to be able to mount an attack outwards, against some powerful person by whom it feels threatened—even if that is a person with whom the ironist also identifies and even if this attack is also in some measure self-directed. However, these minimal boundaries may be lost if identification goes too far. The processes of introjection (taking some aspect of the other person into one's ego and superego) and projection (seeing some aspect of oneself as if it belongs instead to the other person) may become so extensive and so confused that the person loses any clear sense of inside and outside of the self. The aggression that characterizes irony would be beyond the developmental stage of such a person.

When we read *The Trial*, one of our main impressions is of just this kind of extreme confusion between inside and outside. We see this confusion most evidently in the character of Josef K. himself—a good example of it arising early in chapter 1 after Franz and Willem, the two warders, have advised K. to return to his seat and wait, as K. in fact decides to do:

> Es wunderte K., wenigstens aus dem Gedankengang der Wächter wunderte es ihn, daß sie ihn in das Zimmer getrieben und ihn hier allein gelassen hatten, wo er doch zehnfache Möglichkeit hatte sich umzubringen. Gleichzeitig allerdings fragte er sich, mal aus seinem Gedankengang, was für einen Grund er haben könnte, es zu tun . . . Es wäre so sinnlos gewesen sich umzubringen, daß er, selbst wenn er es hätte tun wollen, infolge der Sinnlosigkeit dessen dazu nicht imstande gewesen wäre. Wäre die geistige Beschränktheit der Wächter nicht so auffallend gewesen, so hätte man annehmen können, daß auch sie infolge der gleichen Überzeugung keine Gefahr darin gesehen hätten, ihn allein zu lassen. (17)

[K. was surprised, at least he was surprised considering the warders' point of view, that they had sent him to his room and left him alone there, where he had abundant opportunities to take his life. Though at the same time he also asked himself, looking at it from his own point of view, what possible ground he could have to do so . . . To take his life would be such a senseless act that, even if he wished, he could not bring himself to do it because of its very senselessness. If the intellectual poverty of the warders were not so manifest, he might almost assume that they too saw no danger in leaving him alone, for the very same reason. (8)]

Kernberg's psychotic patient, to whom we have just referred briefly, feared invasion by the thoughts of others. In this passage, we see a related phenomenon: K. prides himself on his ability to leave his own thought process and, by identifying with the warders, to enter directly into their thoughts. (We have also been told on a previous page that K. "wollte sich irgendwie in die Gedanken der Wächter einschleichen, sie zu seinen Gunsten wenden oder sich dort einbürgern" [14-15] [wanted in some way to enter into the thoughts of the warders and twist them to his own advantage or else try to acclimatize himself to them (6)].) K. gives his fantasy a different evaluation than does the psychotic patient, but at base the two fantasies are mirror images of one another. First, neither K. nor the psychotic attributes much weight, substantiality, or opacity to his or her own thoughts. The psychotic believes her thoughts can be nullified by invasion; K., that his thoughts do not anchor him within his own mind. Second, if one reads the above passage for the emotional overtones, one sees quite clearly that K. believes himself to have been suddenly invaded by a thought—the idea that he should kill himself— which appears to K. as if it has come to him from outside himself. Third, we notice with K., as is often the case with psychotics, that the invasive thoughts do not originate from the outside at all. The thought of suicide arises from within K., but K.'s own unconscious attraction to suicide is so frightening and so threatening that he must project the impulse onto his mental image of the warders. But because his internal boundary between his own image of himself and his image of others is so ill defined, this projection fails to protect him from the thoughts he is trying to deny.

One of the areas in which the teachings of psychoanalysis have been most profound concerns a particular double impulse in all human beings. On the one hand, we strive, necessarily, for separation and individuation; on the other, we fear the results of these same processes and seek to nullify the very boundaries that we create between ourselves and others. Identification, with all its complex causes, may generally be seen as an example of the second phenomenon. Normal identifications follow upon the achievement of a certain amount of separation and individuation and, as we have said, would never actually undo the accomplishment of individuation. Pathological identifications, on the other hand, reflect entrapment at a primitive level where individuation has been stalled. This is what we see in the case of Josef K. K. claims that he is able to separate his own train of thought from that of the warders. But the fact is that both trains of thought exist in K.'s own mind and exist there as *equals*. K.'s rationalizing—his belief that he can keep the two separate—covers over an absolute confusion of the two, based upon a pathological identification with these subfigures of authority. K. has no clear idea at all of what belongs to, or originates with, "himself" and what belongs to the authorities.

This extreme confusion between inside and outside is more than simply a feature of K.'s psychology, in that it also seems in some sense to characterize the book as a whole. For *The Trial* presents as "actual" reality what we might think of as K.'s psychotic reality. In normal or normally neurotic human beings, the match between our fantasies of the world and the world that actually impinges upon us can never be complete; we never totally lose our ability to test reality. The psychotic, however, loses precisely this ability. The world he projects upon reality is always the world he finds out there for himself. In *The Trial*, however, not only does K. himself find his paranoid fantasies about the world validated in the world of his experience, but he is right to do so; according to the quasi-omniscient narrative voice we hear, the world of the novel corresponds in fact to what would normally seem to be only someone's psychotic fantasies. Two examples should make this point clear—a small one first: When K. is summoned to the first interrogation (chap. 3 in the new critical edition; chap. 2 in the English translation), he neglects to ask at what time he is expected. Nevertheless, on the day appointed, "lief er jetzt, um nur möglichst um neun Uhr einzutreffen, trotzdem er nicht einmal für eine bestimmte Stunde bestellt war" (52) [he was hurrying so as to arrive by nine o'clock if possible, although he had not even been required to appear at any specified time (34)]. When K. actually arrives, shortly after ten in the morning, he is castigated by the examining magistrate: "Sie hätten vor einer Stunde und fünf Minuten erscheinen sollen" (59) [You should have been here an hour and five minutes ago (38)].

A more critical example comes in the last chapter, when K., not having been told about the arrival of his two executioners, is nevertheless sitting by the door, dressed in black and looking as if he were waiting for visitors. Of course, in this case the fit between K.'s fantasies and the external world is not absolute, since K., disappointed at the comical figures who have called for him, admits to himself "daß er einen andern Besuch erwartet hatte" (305) [that he had been expecting different visitors (223)]. Even in the case of psychosis, Freud and many of his successors have believed, some authentic self can occasionally be glimpsed; the small discrepancy we have noted here between fantasy and reality is simply a momentary flash of this self, which by the time of the last chapter is mostly hidden behind the role K. has taken up as the reasonable man who accepts his punishment.[15] The fate of this self at the very end of the chapter we will discuss below.

The phenomenon we are describing here could be analyzed in a number of ways. For example, The Trial might be thought to represent a dream dreamt by the character Josef K. or even a psychotic fantasy on his part. (The two explanations would, of course, be related, since in Freudian theory a dream is a kind of psychotic state.[16]) Such explanations would allow us to see the book as an imitation of character and would thereby quarantine K.'s pathological inability to distinguish inside from outside. But they would also run counter to our sense that external reality in The Trial is not only an emanation of K.'s psyche but also very real—as well as running counter to our sense of how confused the boundaries are between K. and Kafka. In short, the author himself seems implicated in the psychic state that appears to characterize K., a state in which inner fantasy and outer reality merge with one another. To say this is not necessarily to say anything about Kafka's usual psychic condition, although this condition is certainly viewed by some as having been extraordinarily fragile.[17] But at the very least, one would have to conclude that Kafka in some way is able to regress to a psychological state very near K.'s, with the result that the book represents, as it were, something close to a single psychic level.

We have a novel, then, in which no clear distinction is made between inner and outer world, between "true" reality and "psychotic" reality. Projections and identifications constantly blur any boundaries that the main character (and in some way, the author himself, at least as he exists in his book) might draw around his own ego. In such a book, dominated by the psychological trends we have just described, there could be no verbal irony of the kind we find in *Gulliver's Travels* or even in ordinary everyday discourse. In ordinary irony, the identification between the ironist and her target conceals (unsuccessfully, except in the case of unconscious irony) the underlying aggression; at least in part, this identification accounts for, and is the equivalent to, the surface or literal meaning behind which the true meaning is meant to be discovered. And as we have said, this identification, like the literal level in irony, is often defensive in origin. In *The Trial*, however, identification is scarcely under the control of the ego that wishes to use it for its own purposes. Rather, it signals an insufficiency in the ego, a transparency of the ego to itself. Therefore, when the words of authority are taken over—as they are in irony—they are not subjected to an aggressive critique originating in the ego. Rather, they are taken over as a truth that cannot be withstood. In the "Letter to His Father," we get the impression that Kafka desires the ability to ironize the words of his father and even that he has tried out such irony throughout his life. Unfortunately, he does not have the resistance to his father's words that would be necessary. The same impulse to irony is evident in many parts of *The Trial*, and likewise the same failure.

The difficult game in the "Letter to His Father" comes out particularly at the end, when Kafka gives the floor to his father, ventriloquizing the elder Kafka's response to all that the son has written up to that point. The father is imagined as saying:

> Zuerst lehnst auch Du [i.e., Franz] jede Schuld und Verantwortung von Dir ab, darin ist also unser Verfahren das Gleiche. Während ich aber dann so offen, wie ich es auch meine, die alleinige Schuld Dir zuschreibe, willst Du gleichzeitig "übergescheit" und "überzärtlich" sein und auch mich von jeder Schuld freisprechen. Natürlich gelingt Dir das letztere nur scheinbar (mehr willst Du ja auch nicht) und es ergibt sich zwischen den Zeilen trotz aller "Redensarten" von Wesen und Natur und Gegensatz und Hilflosigkeit, daß eigentlich ich der Angreifer gewesen bin, während alles, was Du getrieben hast,

nur Selbstwehr war. Jetzt hättest Du also schon durch Deine Unaufrichtigkeit genug erreicht, denn Du hast dreierlei bewiesen, erstens daß Du unschuldig bist, zweitens daß ich schuldig bin und drittens daß Du aus lauter Großartigkeit bereit bist, nicht nur mir zu verzeihn, sondern, was mehr und weniger ist, auch noch zu beweisen und es selbst glauben zu wollen, daß ich, allerdings entgegen der Wahrheit, auch unschuldig bin. (214–15)

[First, you (i.e., Franz) too repudiate all guilt and responsibility in this; then, our method is the same. But whereas I then attribute the sole guilt to you as frankly as I mean it, you are at the same time trying to be "too clever" and "too affectionate" and to acquit me of all blame. Of course, in this latter you only apparently succeed (and you do not want more, either), and what appears between the lines, in spite of all the "turns of phrase" about character and nature and antagonism and helplessness, is that actually I have been the aggressor, while everything you were up to was only self-defense. And so for the time being, by means of your insincerity, you would have achieved enough, for you have proved three things, first that you are blameless, secondly that I am to blame, and thirdly that out of sheer magnanimity you are prepared not only to forgive me but, what is both more and less, also to prove, into the bargain, and to try to believe it yourself, that I, contrary to the truth, am also blameless. (194)]

In the "Letter to His Father," Kafka over and over offers up statements that appear to be in ironic form, but their irony is vitiated by the total context in a way that we have examined. In the present passage we see Kafka definitively and retroactively giving up any pretense of irony. Kafka here identifies himself so perfectly with the voice of authority that authority may speak absolutely in its own voice, without ironic subtext, and accurately to boot. Even if Kafka reminds the reader, as he does in the last paragraph of the "Letter to His Father," that he himself is the author of his father's speech, the protest that his own ego is controlling rings hollow. Kafka bows in fear before the authority who recognizes his quasi-ironic attack for what it is, and he retracts the irony by exposing it. One cannot be ironic by giving authority the most telling lines. To make the point in another manner, we can say that irony is basically an attempt to escape responsibility for one's words by having it both ways at once: one both identifies with and attacks the same authority. It is, however, in the interests of authority to cut off this escape by forcing the speaker to be univocal. Thus, when Kafka assigns to his letter one clear meaning—even if this meaning is the aggressive one, the one that threatens his father—he is actually acting against himself, since for Kafka there is certainly no transgression without punishment. Ironic escape, which is normally a neurotic and unsatisfactory solution to the problem of authority, would actually be the best Kafka could hope for. But such an escape would require a self-protective ego that does not seem to be at Kafka's disposal; the wishes of authority seem paramount within Kafka himself. In other words, Kafka's identification with authority is both pathological and masochistic—and incompatible with a successful use of verbal irony.

The same pattern that we see virtually on the surface of the "Letter to His Father" also underlies the psychology of *The Trial*. The hero himself is not capable of resisting his identifications with authority, even though he puts up a continual show of resistance. In fact, we are back to Bergler's concept of 'pseudo-aggression' that attempts to compensate for profound masochistic wishes; the identifications with authority, aside from having a masochistic tinge in themselves (identifying with the aggressor and against oneself), may also serve to cover over the masochistic wishes. Josef K.'s relationship with the merchant Herr Block (chap. 8) exemplifies the various psychological currents we are examining here.

K. has come to visit the lawyer Huld, in fact to dismiss Huld from his case, and while waiting for Leni to announce him to the lawyer, K. gets deep in conversation with Herr Block, a pathetic client of the lawyer; Block is allowed to live in a tiny room off Leni's kitchen while waiting, for days on end, to be received by Huld. Leni returns to find K. and Block talking intimately:

> "Wie Ihr hier beieinander sitzt," rief Leni, die mit der Tasse zurückgekommen war und in der Tür stehen blieb. Sie saßen wirklich eng beisammen, bei der kleinsten Wendung mußten sie mit den Köpfen aneinanderstoßen, der Kaufmann, der abgesehen von seiner Kleinheit auch noch den Rücken gekrümmt hielt, hatte K. gezwungen, sich auch tief zu bücken, wenn er alles hören wollte. (244)
>
> ["How close you've got!" cried Leni, who had come back with the soup bowl and was standing in the doorway. They were indeed sitting so close to each other that they must have bumped their heads together at the slightest movement; Block, who was not only a small man but stooped forward as he sat,

spoke so low that K. was forced to bend down to hear every
word he said. (179)]

K.'s latent impulse to identify himself with someone—anyone—
else has easily been awakened by the similarities between his own
situation and that of this other accused man, so that even though
he initially finds Block repulsive, K. moves psychologically toward
Block in a way brilliantly mirrored by the physical description
here. But subsequently this identification is called into question. K.
is forced to witness an encounter between Block and the lawyer
in which the lawyer displays his power to humiliate the obse-
quious and servile Block. Immediately any conscious identification
between K. and Block is broken, and K. assumes instead an identification with the sadistic and powerful figure of the lawyer. Henceforth, K. views Block from the attitude of someone who has power
over Block, and he is repulsed by this creature who now appears to
him as "der Hund des Advokaten" (265) [the lawyer's dog (193)].
(Part of K.'s horror, of course, must stem from his need to deny his
own, unconsciously persisting, identification with Block.) If K. wit-
nesses an encounter between the helpless child and the omnipotent
adult, his conscious identification can lie only with the adult.

By contrast, we note that it is the servile Block who has the
inner resistance that might fund an ironic attack on authority.
Block plays up to the lawyer, even debasing himself in front of
Huld, but he remains separate from this figure of authority. He
does not show the same confused identification with authority
that so totally undermines K.'s sense of his own ego. Thus, Block
has hired other lawyers, disreputable ones even, in addition to
Huld, and he does everything he can to conceal this fact from his
lawyer. He may not have the courage to openly attack Huld, but
he is willing to carry on a secret revolt. One might even claim that
Block's performance as "the lawyer's dog" shows, in its dramatic
extremism, signs of the kind of unconscious irony we have noted
elsewhere. It is quite clear that Block, who has managed to drag
his trial out for five long years, is capable of something that K.
himself, executed after but a year, can scarcely accomplish. Block
can remain in the limbo of unresolved ambivalence, and neither
his subservience nor his rebelliousness can win a clear victory—a
victory that, in the scheme of The Trial, would represent a final
outcome to Block's own trial. Put another way, neither Block's
ego (his "self") nor his superego (the voice of authority) is able to

put an end to his ambivalence. Block remains in what we have recognized to be the domain of irony. K., on the other hand, represents a far more complicated case. He is as rebellious as Block—after all, he goes to the lawyer Huld to take him off the case—but Kafka seems to present all of K.'s rebellions as pathetic efforts whose futility dooms them from the start. Kafka never finished the chapter we are discussing, so he never tells us for sure whether K. succeeds in firing his lawyer. But we can be certain of one thing: if K. does fire the lawyer, this action cannot prevent K. from taking on, through identification with the lawyer and all the other authorities of the court, the inhuman (and also, as psychoanalysis reminds us, the all too human) judgment of the court. He might try to escape this identification by firing his lawyer, but the feeble protest does not succeed. "Independently" of each other, K. and the court reach the same verdict at the same time, and K. acquiesces in it even to the point of his own annihilation. If irony results from an unresolvable ambivalence between the "self" and the internal successors to the powerful authorities of childhood, between hostile rebellion and self-effacing submission (in which the ironist even purports to speak in the voice of the authority), then we can see easily enough why the irony of *The Trial* seems blighted. For the action of *The Trial*, though it represents ambivalence at every step—indeed, nowhere more so than on the last page of the novel—nevertheless moves in an underlying direction that symbolizes the resolution of ambivalence.

Psychoanalysis teaches us that however harmful neurotic symptoms may seem to be in the life of a human being, they often represent a significant, even lifesaving achievement. For they may defend against forces internal or external with which a person simply cannot coexist. Often the neurotic symptoms are no longer appropriate from a realistic point of view; the threat has disappeared (or in reality may never have been present at all), but the neurosis persists to the needless cost of the individual. Sometimes, however, the symptom, or some substitute symptom, remains necessary for the person simply to continue to exist, even if that existence is severely limited by the symptoms themselves. What we see in *The Trial* is a dissolution, masking as a resolution, of a neurotic ambivalence of the kind normally associated with obsessive-compulsive neuroses. And the result is disastrous. For the dissolution is not liberating (as psychoanalytic theory hopes that its therapy can be); instead, Josef K. sacrifices his self in favor of the tyrannical demands of authority. In other words, Josef K. the character would have been better off to remain, like Block, in a permanent state of ambivalence; at least the ambivalence preserved in some form the claims of the self.

How we are to relate Josef K.'s fate with the psychology of Kafka himself is, of course, an impossible question to answer satisfactorily. Nevertheless, we can scarcely fail to note that the last chapter, which describes K.'s execution, assumes much of the character of a wish-fulfillment fantasy. Part of the wish, certainly, is the desire to escape from the perpetual stasis of the obsessive-compulsive neurosis, or rather the perpetual to and fro, as in the case of the man who, on going to bed, would turn his shoes first parallel to the bed, then perpendicular, then back, and so on until he would simply fall asleep from exhaustion. Absent this desire, K.'s trial would continue indefinitely, never getting any closer to an outcome than it was on the very first day. But from the point of view of psychic health, the wished-for escape goes in the wrong direction: Kafka's escape is the self-immolation of a punishment fantasy. How different in tonality this is from the "resolution" at the end of *Gulliver's Travels*. Ambivalence comes to an end at the conclusion of Swift's book, too, but it is resolved into Gulliver's furious universal misanthropy. This misanthropy has a strong undercurrent of masochism, not only because it must, after all, be unconsciously directed at Gulliver himself, a human being like the rest of his odious race, but also because it serves to isolate him almost completely from his wife and children, his friends, and all other humans. Gulliver has put himself into solitary confinement. Still, all of this happens under the guise of an aggressive stance, Gulliver thrusting away the rest of the world as unworthy. At the end of *The Trial*, on the other hand, the masochistic fantasy is essentially passive, and it shows K. trying to make himself absolutely at one with the very authorities who wish to murder him. The erotic wish to be at one with the father and also to be stabbed with his threatening knife predominates in the imaginer of this fantasy.

THE IRONY OF THE FATHER

By putting together evidence from both *The Trial* and the more explicitly autobiographical "Letter to His Father," we have been able to sketch out two trends to Kafka's irony as it appears in *The*

Trial. First, Kafka successfully suppresses—defuses, covers over, flattens, draws back from—a pronounced tendency to ironic statement, and he does so for the obvious reason that irony unconsciously strikes him as very dangerous. One of irony's most pressing dangers is the fear of retaliation by the father or by the authorities (including the superego) who are the father's psychic descendants and the intended victims of the ironic attack. For most ironists, the screen offered by the literal level of an ironic attack provides the unconscious with enough protection to allow for the dangerous attack to proceed. Kafka, however, is bedeviled by too great a fear to admit this kind of ambivalent compromise-formation. He must not only disguise his attack through irony but must even seem to disavow the irony itself. Second, Kafka also resists his own tendency to irony because he over-identifies with the authorities he is attacking, and therefore he cannot sustain his belief that he is right and good and they are wrong and bad—and deserve to be attacked. Again, identification with the authorities being attacked is a crucial part of the ambivalence characteristic of *any* ironic statement. But Kafka's extreme version of this identification takes him outside the psychic band in which ordinary verbal irony normally exists.

We now come to a third trend, and this one, too, we will first approach through Kafka's "Letter to His Father." We want to explore one further source of Kafka's fear of irony, one suggested by an autobiographical fact to be found in the "Letter." Kafka writes of his father: "Ein besonders Vertrauen hattest Du zur Erziehung durch Ironie, sie entsprach auch am besten Deiner Überlegenheit über mich" (162) [You put special trust in bringing children up by means of irony, and this was most in keeping with your superiority over me (153)]. Kafka explains:

> Eine Ermahnung hatte bei Dir gewöhnlich diese Form: "Kannst Du das nicht so und so machen? Das ist Dir wohl schon zu viel? Dazu hast Du natürlich keine Zeit?" und ähnlich. Dabei jede solche Frage begleitet von bösem Lachen und bösem Gesicht. Man wurde gewissermaßen schon bestraft, ehe man noch wußte, daß man etwas Schlechtes getan hatte. Aufreizend waren auch jene Zurechtweisungen, wo man als dritte Person behandelt, also nicht einmal des bösen Ansprechens gewürdigt wurde; wo Du also etwa formell zur Mutter sprachst, aber eigentlich zu mir, der dabei saß, z.B.: "Das kann man vom Herrn Sohn natürlich nicht haben" und dgl. (162)

[An admonition from you generally took this form: "Can't you do it in such-and-such a way? That's too hard for you, I suppose. You haven't the time, of course?" and so on. And each such question would be accompanied by malicious laughter and a malicious face. One was so to speak already punished before one even knew that one had done something bad. What was also maddening were those rebukes when one was treated as a third person, in other words accounted not worthy even to be spoken to angrily: that is to say, when you would speak in form to Mother but in fact to me, sitting there at the same time. For instance: "Of course, that's too much to expect of our worthy son" and the like. (153)]

This passage gives us yet another hint as to why irony became exceptionally dangerous to Franz Kafka. As a general rule, when the young child develops her ability to ironically imitate the adults around her, either in gestures or in words, she seems to believe that she has discovered or invented, on her own, a secret language that the powerful adult cannot penetrate. This process is well described in a case history reported by H. Schneider. Schneider speaks here of his patient "Ernst A.":

He still recalled how he resented the fact that his mother showed a submissive attitude toward his father, and especially that she would leave her son, the patient, to fend for himself when he was attacked by his father. As a small boy, he feared his father; later he became contemptuous. He began to mock his father, at first when the father was not present, later even when he was. The patient did this in such a way that his father noticed nothing, while his mother, who had a more sensitive ear, did not forbid the boy's behavior. Ernst believed that his mother had even taken a secret pleasure in it. In this manner Ernst had become his mother's ally, or even her accomplice, against his father, whose rigidity and severity appeared all the more comical the more he was made an object of mockery. At the same time that Ernst developed his talent for mockery, which over the years took on ever more subtle, sharply ironic forms, he became more and more sensitive. It had finally become a characteristic of the adult patient that he would react immoderately to even the smallest offense. Not that he could have shown this reaction on the spot—but he wouldn't get over it for weeks, would be exceptionally resentful, and would avenge himself, in his way, at the first opportunity, by trying to take care of the offender with mocking irony.[18]

I have quoted Schneider at length because of the inherent interest this description has for the psychology of irony, but for the moment let me simply emphasize that the young boy seems to have hit spontaneously upon this solution to his problem: the invention of ironic utterance as a way of expressing contempt, before an audience, while not exposing himself directly to the object of his fearful contempt. (Notice, too, that Ernst A. remembers the resentment he felt at his *mother's* submissiveness. We may assume, however, that his real anger was unconsciously directed at his own submissiveness to the father and that the patient's concealed aggressiveness was, and continues to be, more an attempt to *deny* the basic reality of his submissiveness than an effective attempt to change this basic reality.) Kafka, too, in a passage from the "Letter to His Father" quoted above, implies a similar spontaneous development: "Um mich Dir gegenüber nur ein wenig zu behaupten, zum Teil auch aus einer Art Rache, fing ich bald an, kleine Lächerlichkeiten, die ich an Dir bemerkte, zu beobachten, zu sammeln, zu übertreiben" (166) [In order to assert myself a little in relation to you, and partly too from a kind of vengefulness, I soon began to observe little ridiculous things about you, collecting them and exaggerating them (156)]. Ernst A., however, had one significant advantage over the young Franz Kafka. Ernst's father was deaf to the boy's irony, which was thereby every bit as safe as the young mind that invented it could wish it to be; indeed, Ernst A. even achieves—or thinks he achieves—an oedipal triumph, believing that his revenge over his father is accepted as a pleasurable gift by the boy's submissive mother.

Kafka, on the other hand, had no such luck with his father, who at least on occasion noticed what Franz was up to when he would ironically exaggerate his father's weaknesses: "Du bemerktest es manchmal, ärgertest Dich darüber, hieltest es für Bosheit, Respektlosigkeit" (166) [you sometimes noticed it and were angry about it, taking it to be malice and lack of respect for you (156)]. But even worse, I believe, than the fact that Kafka's father would occasionally see through Franz's ironic dissimulation was the fact that the father himself would resort to irony as a way to chasten his son. Irony, the weapon "invented" by the weak child as "revenge" against the powerful father, turns out to belong to the arsenal of the father himself and indeed to be employed, with more force than the child could ever muster, against this same child. The result, we may speculate, would be twofold. First, the secret weapon of the child has been badly compromised; it is dangerous to use because it does not conceal the intention it was designed to conceal and also because the same weapon may be turned back crushingly on the child who employs it. On the other hand, the second result would seem to work in a contrary direction. The boy, that is, would tend to identify with the aggressor, with the father who uses irony to chastize and humiliate this son, and consequently he would tend to employ this same irony himself. This irony could be directed outwards, just as the father's was, but it could also be directed against the child himself. For the child, in identifying with the powerful aggressor, may go so far in his mimicry as to select the same victim as did the adult—that is, the child himself. In this case, the ironic attack on the self would emanate from the superego, the descendant within the child of the aggressive adult with whom the child has identified. This result gives us a new danger associated with irony: When the child uses irony as a form of attack, just as the powerful adult did, he may find that he is still himself the victim.[19]

This hypothesis seems plausible when we are speaking about Kafka and a novel like *The Trial*. For we may certainly say of the novel that all of its aspects emanate, in a particularly monomaniacal fashion, from a single psyche and that there is little in the novel that has any independence apart from that psyche. Therefore, no aggression, no attack, be it ironical or in some other form, can reach the outside—or can even be plausibly directed toward the outside; it must necessarily turn back upon this single psyche. The same kind of statement could undoubtedly be made about the plot of Kafka's life itself and would perhaps be more true about that life than about many others. Kafka was certainly aware of this trend in his own psyche, and he would have had to realize, consciously or unconsciously, that any ironic attack he launched could effectively have only one target; hence, irony would necessarily appear as a very dangerous weapon for this reason as well.

A curious dream that Kafka reports in a letter to Milena Jesenská (probably from 1920) sheds further light on some of the unconscious attitudes that we have been examining here:

Jemand, ein Verwandter, sagte im Verlauf eines Gespräches, an das ich mich nicht erinnere, das aber etwa den Sinn hatte, daß irgendetwas dieser und jener nicht zustandebringen könnte—ein

Verwandter sagte also schließlich ironisch: "Dann also vielleicht Milena." Darauf ermordete ich ihn irgendwie, kam dann aufgeregt nachhause, die Mutter lief immerfort hinter mir, es war auch hier ein ähnliches Gespräch im Gang; schließlich schrie ich heiß vor Wut: "Wenn jemand Milena im Bösen nennt, zum Beispiel der Vater (mein Vater), ermorde ich auch ihn oder mich."

[Someone, a relative, said in the course of a conversation which I don't remember but which had more or less the meaning that this or that person couldn't accomplish something— thus this relative said ironically at last: "Well, then perhaps Milena." Whereupon I killed him somehow, came home in great excitement, my mother running after me all the time, here too a similar conversation was taking place; at last hot with rage I cried out: "If anyone says anything bad about Milena, for instance the father (my father), I'll kill him too or myself."][20]

An ironic attack is launched by an unspecified relative on a woman with whom Kafka is having a kind of affair. Obviously there is an identification here between Kafka and Milena, one that is confirmed by the shift in scene to Kafka's home and by the nature of the charge. For the relative sounds like a parent who is accusing his child of never accomplishing anything; indeed, the accusation is simply a stronger version of the ironic mockery aimed at Kafka by his father and described in the "Letter to His Father." In the dream, Kafka tries to strangle the irony by murdering the relative, but despite his exhilaration, the irony seems ready to break out once more. The only chance he has to kill the irony is to confront its ultimate source, the original relative from whom it derives—the father's quintessential role being slightly disguised in the dream by the "for instance." But the very thought of killing the father immediately leads to the terrible "or": Kafka must kill himself instead; only thereby can the irony that has been loosed on the world be definitively destroyed, as if irony had come into existence to punish Kafka and will go out of existence only when the punishment has been executed. And in typical Kafkaesque fashion, the dreamer must inflict the punishment on himself, either as the sacrifical lamb or as the guilty son whose transgressions have brought this curse, irony, into being (or as both). But of course there is another twist to the plot of Kafka's dream, for the "or" also reveals an identification between Kafka and his father; indeed, in the dream Kafka may have substituted

Milena for himself not only to avoid arousing greater anxiety (if he were the direct target of the attack) but also to allow the strange double identification with both victim and aggressor. In the case of the latter identification, Kafka still needs to rid this dream world of irony—his interests as the target of irony seem controlling—but now he is an ironist, like the father, and must fall victim to the victim's rage.

This second identification in Kafka's dream suggests a slightly different direction in which we must develop the observation that Kafka associated irony with his father. As the psychoanalyst Ralph R. Greenson points out, a person's hatred, and total rejection, of a powerful figure from his childhood world often covers over a deep-seated identification with that figure and, in fact, represents a struggle against that identification.[21] And, of course, observable traits of behavior are often signs of a conscious or unconscious identification. Thus, if Kafka's attempt to distance himself from his father is an attempt to deny a hated, but real, identification with his father, then we can see another source for Kafka's deep ambivalence about irony. The identification with the father would naturally express itself by the son's use of the father's characteristic irony, while the wish to disavow the identification would render irony unusable for the son. There are, of course, many ways to express an ambivalence of this kind. For example, a person might use ironic expression but remain unconscious of the fact that he is doing so; he would, in other words, be using denial or repression. Or a person might, sequentially and repeatedly, use irony and then attempt to retract or apologize for the ironic statement; in this case, he would be trying to "undo" the irony about the use of which he feels ambivalent. In *The Trial*, at least, Kafka uses yet a third method for expressing his ambivalence. As I have tried to show, he writes passages that exhibit the superficial form of verbal irony but at the same time lack a certain ironic tone, as if the necessary affect had been left out. This kind of solution we can think of as a compromise formation. What we get is something that is partly irony and partly a retreat from irony; both sides of the ambivalence—the wish and the aversion (or fear)—are present simultaneously and contribute to the actual expression that results from their conflict. The end product is necessarily elusive, for irony itself, as it ordinarily appears, is already a compromise formation.

Given this elusiveness, there can be little biographical evidence that in his everyday life Kafka used irony in the sort of ambivalent way we have been discussing. However, in recalling Kafka's affair with a barmaid named Hansi, Max Brod does offer a pertinent reminiscence: "An entry in my diary runs: 'Trocadero wine bar. There he [Franz] is in love with a Germania from the German postal stamps, *chambre séparée*. But he is so extraordinarily shy. When he says, "I'll pay your rent for you," he laughs as if he meant it ironically.'"22 What we see here, through Brod's eyes, is what we have also found in *The Trial*: an ironic form that somehow, and confusingly, seems to lack an ironic intention.

IRONY AND SELF-DAMAGE

In accordance with the psychoanalytic notion of overdetermination (psychic "results" tend to have many causes, at least some of which might in themselves have been sufficient causes), we have explored a number of explanations for Kafka's curious relation to irony in *The Trial*. But it also seems to me that at the basis of all these various explanations lies a fundamental trend in Kafka's psychic life, one that accounts for his efforts to draw back from irony in the novel we are considering and also illuminates much about the psychic sources of irony in general. This fundamental trend can be seen easily enough in the very structure of *The Trial*, at the center of which we can see the masochistic desire to damage and to punish oneself. This desire clearly belongs to the character Josef K. (and presumably also to Kafka himself), and it is the motive force that launches and pushes forward his year-long trial; it culminates in the immolation fantasy with which the novel ends. As we now know from Malcolm Pasley's work on the *Trial* manuscript, Kafka wrote the concluding chapter after he had finished the opening section, "Verhaftung" [The Arrest] and before any of the intervening sections were composed, so this end point, the execution/suicide, was predetermined in the highest degree.23 And yet, one could argue that the novel as a whole does not represent a suicide fantasy—the ultimate masochistic fantasy of self-damage—although it ends with such a fantasy. Rather, the novel focuses on Josef K.'s attempts to deny and resist his masochistic drives, and it is shaped as a sustained effort to resist the concluding fantasy, to avoid giving in to it. Indeed, the episodic structure of the novel represents the possibility that the struggle between masochistic desires and the wish to resist them could be prolonged indefinitely. Kafka himself seems to have hinted at this aspect of the novel, as we learn from Max Brod's "Postscript" to the first edition of *The Trial*: "Franz regarded the novel as unfinished. Before the final chapter given here a few more stages of the mysterious trial were to have been described. But as the trial, according to the author's own statement made by word of mouth, was never to get as far as the highest court, in a certain sense the novel could never be terminated—that is to say, it could be prolonged into infinity" (271).[24]

As the novel now stands, the concluding chapter arrives abruptly, and its tone and its presentation of Josef K.'s frame of mind differ sharply from what has preceded; to reestablish continuity, we have to do considerable interpreting in order to hypothesize what has transpired in the gap between the next-to-last and the last chapters. Naturally, one is tempted to think that what we have is an unfinished work and that if Kafka had finished the chapters that were to intervene between what are presently the two last chapters, then the break in continuity would have been filled in by Kafka himself. I would suggest, however—like Brod, but for different reasons—that no continuity could ever have been established. In the above quotation, Brod portrays the novel as a version of Zeno's paradox on account of the logic of the plot; but he ignores the fact that *The Trial* does reach an end, even if in some sense the novel is unfinished. A psychological, rather than a narratological, explanation would perhaps better account for the break between the final chapter and the preceding ones: When Kafka, like his hero Josef K., can no longer sustain the effort of resisting his frightening, overwhelming masochistic impulses, he simply gives in to the ultimate masochistic fantasy. In the case of the writer, this fantasy lies ready to hand, in one of his notebooks, there to assume its place as a conclusion whenever the writer's energy fails or when he despairs of resisting it; Kafka is both a Scheherazade who cannot spin his tales for a thousand and one nights and the sultan who exacts the penalty.

Let us now recall Edmund Bergler's argument that the main way a person fights his own masochistic, self-damaging wishes is by engaging in shows of "pseudo-aggression" directed outward. These shows serve to "prove" to the individual that he is not in fact guilty of harboring masochistic wishes. (For Bergler, as in a sense for "humanistic" psychoanalysts, our deepest guilt results from awareness of our own desire to harm ourselves.) Such pseudo-aggression—that is, aggression for its own sake, aggression that does not really serve to promote our interests—certainly appears throughout *The Trial*, especially in Josef K.'s feisty but useless combativeness, most evident perhaps during his Sunday interrogation before the crowd at the law courts. Indeed, the very manner in which Kafka frames the basic struggle of the book, as a battle between his hero Josef K. and the hostile powers of the court, tends to reveal the novel as itself an act of pseudo-aggression. One might wonder, then, why irony is refused as an offensive weapon in the book, especially when Kafka seems so inclined by nature to use it.

The answer lies in the fact that Kafka is necessarily sensitive to anything that might bring to consciousness the guilty masochistic wishes that he is trying so hard to repress by means of his pseudo-aggression or any other mechanism of denial. To be sure, Kafka is far too self-aware to keep anything from his consciousness for very long, and the struggle to repress masochistic wishes—a struggle portrayed now within the character of Josef K.—becomes, in fact, an overt theme of the novel. We may think, for example, of the punishment fantasy that makes up the chapter "Der Prügler" [The Whipper]. On hearing muffled screams, Josef K. opens the door of a storeroom in his office building—even at work he cannot escape his besetting fantasies—and discovers Franz and Willem, the two warders who first arrested him, being whipped because K. has complained about their behavior during his arrest. But K., who is responsible for their punishment (though he of course tries to deny this), also begins to identify with the victims, and it is this identification that he must fight—by attempting to identify instead with the punishing authorities—if he is to continue to repress his own wishes. Finally, he must simply flee, slamming the door on this enactment of his own masochistic fantasy. He turns his back on the struggle that is actually consuming him and goes off in a different direction to tilt at windmills. Of course, on some continuum of self-consciousness, Kafka himself is much further along than is Josef K. But—and this is the source of the inexhaustible truthfulness of the novel—Kafka still exists on this very same continuum with the character Josef K., and his superiority to K. is only relative; he in no sense exists in a different order of knowledge and understanding, as do the omniscient authors of literary theory. So even if Kafka is much more aware of his masochistic wishes than is Josef K., he too struggles against them by attempts at repression—in a way that psychoanalysis, of course, finds counterproductive and harmful, though inevitable. When by default he indulges these wishes, in fantasy, by yielding to the already-written immolation scene that ends *The Trial*, he is giving up his fight to repress, though of course he has also gained no victory over the tormenting wishes. Up to that point, however, as long as he is engaging in the effort to keep his own masochism from consciousness (or to remove it whenever it appears there, as when he writes the execution scene and then retreats from it), then he, like Josef K., will necessarily remain extremely sensitive to anything that might remind him of, or confirm, his desire for self-punishment.

Irony, necessarily, would be such a reminder. For, as we have emphasized previously, the use of irony always involves a greater or lesser amount of self-damage. At the very least, the ironist pretends to divest himself of his adult knowledge and adult powers. But a psychoanalytic viewpoint requires us to see that this pretense is not without meaning. It enacts, in however attenuated a fashion, the wish to regress to the much less dangerous state of childhood—a state in which the ironist will not be attacked (or counterattacked) by the powerful adults, because he represents no real threat to them. This pretense also requires and symbolically enacts the same feared punishment that a more powerful authority might inflict on the ironist—the obliteration of adult (sexual) knowledge and power—except that the punishment is carried out by the ironist himself. And like other attempts at self-punishment, it is motivated to a significant extent by the wish for expiation: if the ironist is going to attack the feared authority, he had better at the same time try to propitiate the authority by offering as a sacrifice his own self-punishment. He especially hopes that this self-punishment will prevent the authority from exacting an even more brutal price—castration and death, as psychoanalysis formulates the ultimate punishment.[25]

This self-punishing, masochistic element may, I believe, be found in all irony, even relatively "innocent" or "harmless" examples like the first one analyzed in chapter 1 ("Why, I didn't know you knew shorthand!"). But certainly there are instances of irony when this element is much more prominent and more visible than in others. In such cases, we often speak of "self-deprecating" irony; an example of this would be the passage from Freud's letter to Reik that was examined in chapter 1 ("I am ready to help you as soon as I get the news that I am equipped with the omnipotence of God, if only for a short time. Until then, you must continue to toil alone"). The masochistic element in self-deprecating irony often goes beyond the self-damaging regression inherent in all irony, and it would tend to include as well stronger attacks on the self that derive from the superego. For example, Freud's remark is not only an overt criticism of Reik's whining importunities but also a (somewhat concealed) criticism of Freud's own repressed fantasies of omnipotence. Kafka, we have speculated, would certainly have expected his irony to take this "self-deprecating" turn, especially because of his own particular experience with irony, when as a boy he was the victim of his father's ironic attacks.

But why would irony tend to add this self-deprecating element to the inherent masochistic regression? For an answer, we can look only to the psychoanalytic theory that all human beings have a fund of masochistic impulses that will seek to find expression in one way or another. Freud, of course, ultimately founds this theory on his infamous hypothesis of a "death instinct," but his successors have not always chosen to go that far with him. We might simply stay with a statement such as the following one by the psychoanalyst Charles Brenner: "Masochism is a normal component or characteristic of the human personality, as witness the part it plays in superego formation and functioning."[26] It then makes sense to suppose that these masochistic wishes would seek to overwhelm the defenses of the ego precisely when they have already won a limited outlet or expression of some kind, when they have, as it were, already breached the self-protecting defenses of the ego. Because irony involves, in however limited a degree, just this kind of self-damage to the ego, it becomes a natural vehicle for even more vehement forms of masochistic expression. Moreover, since irony also involves an attack against the powerful adults of childhood, it will provoke concurrently an especially great need for expiatory self-punishment; this need can be met by the excesses of self-deprecatory irony. We can perhaps best see this latter connection, between the need to propitiate the parents and the masochistic element of irony, if we recall, not an instance of self-deprecating irony, but the unconscious irony of an obsessive-compulsive symptom. In Reik's suggestive case study of the young nobleman who was tormented by obsessive thoughts, Reik demonstrated that these thoughts (e.g., that people of the lower classes were subhuman devils) could be analyzed as ironic attacks on his parents' teachings. But the patient could not attack his parents without simultaneously paying an extremely high price, which we should undoubtedly view as expiatory or propitiatory. The price, of course, was the torment of the obsessional thoughts themselves, and indeed the patient inflicted much more damage on himself than his obscurely ironical attacks could possibly have inflicted on his parents, even if the parents were still living and capable of helplessly witnessing their son's obsessional neurosis.

The irony of Reik's patient does not, of course, fall within the range of ordinary verbal irony. The proportions are different. The patient's irony remains unconscious, presumably because his fear of attacking his parents is so great that the attacks—which are, despite the fear, still carried out—cannot become conscious. The ordinary verbal ironist, on the other hand, is at least aware that he is attacking something. Furthermore, Reik's patient pays a much higher price for his extremely attenuated criticism than the ordinary ironist does for more overt (though still somewhat disguised) attacks. But even the ordinary ironist pays his blood money.

We conclude, then, that the ironist—whether the ordinary verbal ironist or even Reik's ironic obsessive—acts out, and even augments, his masochistic impulses in the very use of ironic expression. But we may speculate that he remains largely indifferent to the part masochism plays in his irony. Indeed—and this is what the example of Kafka helps us to understand—if the ironist *were* sensitive to the extent masochism was involved in his irony, he would find himself choking off the irony just as we see Kafka doing in *The Trial*. Here we are again relying on Bergler's idea that masochism is, to the human psyche, the gravest of all crimes—an idea that harmonizes, one might add, with the venerable Western thesis that self-preservation is the first law of nature. Thus, if the individual becomes aware of his own masochism, then it is against this masochism that he must direct his primary struggle. His primary resistance, whether successful or not, would be targeted against manifestations of this masochism. Since irony, as we have shown, necessarily involves a significant masochistic element, then this individual could not freely give in to his inclination to express himself through irony. And what we find in the case of Kafka's *Trial* is that when the impulse to irony is resisted, then the naturalness of the irony is impaired (a "naturalness" arising from irony's source in deeply unconscious processes), and the ironic effect is more or less lost. The successful ironist, on the other hand, is successful precisely because he remains largely unaware of the masochistic component of his irony. He believes that he is directing his aggression outward and remains oblivious to the high price in masochistic self-damage that he is paying for this attack—a price especially high in light of the generally ineffectual nature of aggression through verbal irony. He is not disturbed in his belief that the battle he is fighting is between himself and the outer world.

A broad comparison between the author-character relationship in *Gulliver's Travels* and *The Trial* should make this point clear. The heroes of the two novels figure in a series of well-defined fictional adventures, such that both characters seem to have earned the right to be considered as personages apart from their creators. Psychologically, however, neither character exists separately from his creator; each is in some sense a stand-in for the book's author. Swift, at the deepest level, acknowledges this fusion by sharing his "I" with his character Lemuel Gulliver. But in addition to using Gulliver as his mouthpiece for outward-directed ironic attacks, Swift also makes Gulliver himself into an object of ironic abuse. Swift is thereby indulging in a quite overt form of masochism. And yet, despite this psychologically almost self-evident proposition, the masochistic element is hard to find on the surface of the book; it is more an undercurrent available to analysis than it is an emotional affect belonging to the book. Something, indeed, has worked very hard to efface it. What we are seeing—for Swift's book is as true as Kafka's—is an illustration of that very process of denial that is so central to certain forms of neurotic repression. That is to say, Swift quite clearly shows us (and himself) the self-damaging, self-mocking impulses that he simultaneously manages to deny as being directed at himself. Though Gulliver speaks with Swift's "I," Gulliver seems to us, and to Swift, to be someone other than Swift. In the face of all the evidence to the contrary, Swift puts across the fiction that his ironic aggression is aimed toward the outside, away from Swift himself. This fiction, I have maintained, is necessary for the sustained production of verbal irony. Still, *we* should not forget—just because Swift more or less manages to do so—that it is indeed a fiction created in the service of denial and as a means of psychological repression. We should not close our eyes to the psychological realities just because we have grown accustomed to the methodological (or rather, pedagogical) assumption that the persona is separate from the author.[27] Let us, rather, acknowledge that the availability of a persona, a character who both is and is not the author, as one of the standard resources of literature gives to writers an almost unique way of repressing dangerous wishes while at the same time indulging and displaying them. Swift surely uses Gulliver in this way, especially to disguise the masochistic impulses that he plays out via his hero Gulliver. And Swift's relatively successful denial of his own masochism is a necessary correlate of his continuing ability throughout *Gulliver's Travels* to stay on the offensive and to use verbal irony as one of his weapons of choice.

As we have already implied, Kafka really moves in the opposite direction from Swift. When Swift uses formal devices such as the first-person speaker that would apparently identify himself and Gulliver, he is engaging in bravado, much like what the psychoanalysts call "counter-phobic behavior" (which occurs when a person does something that unconsciously terrifies him in order to convince himself that he is not afraid). Swift flirts with a masochistic identification in order to show that it means nothing to him. Kafka, on the other hand, first of all acknowledges the true relationship, by baldly naming his protagonist "Josef K." (just as he acknowledges his connection with the warder Franz, a connection he tries to flee in the "Whipper" chapter); but at the same time he uses formal devices—a third-person narrative delivered by the most faceless of narrators—that would distance him from his main character. The masochistic identification with *his* main character is such a clear and present danger that Kafka must flee it in every way he can—even as he seems to be confessing it openly. Kafka's efforts are futile, of course; even the traditionally distancing narrative form becomes contaminated with the feared identification. But the point is that Kafka is far too aware of the danger to be able to toy with it, to flout it, in the cavalier way Swift does. Kafka can scarcely deny his masochistic wishes as Swift does, and therefore he is unable to ignore the danger that any use of irony would pose to himself.

CHAPTER 4

Swift, Kafka, and the Origins of Irony

In the chapter on Swift we have shown at length how the fantasies imbedded in the plot of the novel, particularly as they are enacted in "A Voyage to Lilliput," reveal the psychological underpinnings for the irony that runs throughout *Gulliver's Travels*. But to a remarkable extent much of the same plot is played out in Kafka's novel as well. And even though the irony of *The Trial* is ultimately blighted, the impulse to irony is evidently a strong force in the novel. Hence, it will be worthwhile to focus explicitly on those aspects of *The Trial* that may be related to plot elements important for understanding the irony of *Gulliver's Travels*. This comparison will help us to summarize what we have had to say about the psychological underpinnings, and even origins, of irony, and will serve as a conclusion to the present study.

To begin with, there is the matter of food. In the prehistory of *The Trial*, Josef K. was fed promptly and lovingly by his "mother"—the landlady Frau Grubach or her stand-in, Anna the cook. The novel opens precisely at the moment when Anna fails, one morning, to bring K. his breakfast. Instead, the very warders who arrest K. eat up his breakfast and offer to buy him another from the café across the street if he will pay for the breakfast. What has happened is that K.'s access to food, and hence to the most fundamental instinctual gratification, is for the moment controlled by the punishing authorities, rather than being dispensed by the bountiful and freely giving mother. In fact, there is even competition between K. and the authorities for this food. The same contamination of food by authority occurs virtually at the beginning of *Gulliver's Travels*. Gulliver, helpless to feed himself, receives his food through the dispensation of the emperor (again, not the loving mother), and as a condition for being fed he must acknowledge the emperor's authority over him and must agree to the emperor's strictures on his behavior.

We see here the origin of that ambivalent attitude toward authority that is one of the most characteristic features of the obsessive-compulsive and that also, both in *Gulliver's Travels* and *The Trial*, underlies the impulse to irony. If authority can control the helpless child's access to the most basic of needs and gratifications, then naturally this authority is feared and hated on account of its power, and the urge to rebel is strong. On the other hand, the authority has far too much power for the child to risk an open rebellion. At the very least, lip service must be paid. At most, the child will be so frightened that even the wish to rebel has to be repressed from consciousness; indeed, total identification with the hated authority may at the conscious level take the place of this wish. In the obsessive-compulsive neurotic, the psychoanalyst normally sees this almost total repression. In his symptoms, the compulsive acts out the alternation between two wishes: between the impulse to attack the hated authority, on the one hand, and the desire to deny, or undo, or atone for this very aggression, on the other. And the alternation itself between these two impulses takes place under such severe repression that they are expressed only through obliquely symbolic acts whose meaning is for the most part unknown to the person performing them.

In irony, as compared to display of obsessive symptoms, the temporal alternation is collapsed, and the two alternative wishes may be expressed simultaneously. Two possibilities then arise. The first case is similar to that of the obsessive whose fear is so great that he remains unaware of half of his ambivalence, that is, of the wish to attack the powerful authority. In this case we see what might be called "*unconscious* irony." The surface, or literal, level—which in irony is always the one that repeats or borrows the words of authority—reveals the only meaning *consciously* intended by the ironist. The ironist's words admit of another, subversive meaning, which of course is not random or accidental but has been generated with malicious intention by the typical opportunistic brilliance of the unconscious—but of this the ironist may remain unaware. The conscious identification with authority remains undisturbed.

In the second case, that of ordinary, conscious verbal irony, there is still a certain amount of repression touching one of the two conflicting wishes that seek to achieve simultaneous expression through a single utterance. Oddly enough, however, this repression aims at the submissive, passive wishes, those by which the ironist identifies with the powerful and punishing adult, those that are ultimately associated with expiatory and masochistic impulses. Thus, it is the *surface* level of the ironic statement—the level that repeats the words of authority—that actually represents the repressed wish. Moreover, if the ironist is to successfully repress in his own consciousness the psychic meaning belonging to the overt level of his ironic statement, he must naturally render this meaning more or less invisible to himself—and in the process, more or less invisible to those who hear him. It is no wonder, then, though this result seems paradoxical, that we tend to look through or past the literal level of irony, that we so rarely see what meaning this level could possibly have in itself or what meaning it might represent in the conflicted psyche of the ironist. Irony is a device that allows the ironist to express both his rebellious, aggressive wishes and his submissive, masochistic ones—while more or less concealing the latter from himself and from others. As in the case of Poe's purloined letter, the ironist places right in front of us what is to be concealed, and she tempts us—and herself—to look in a secret hiding place for the meaning of her statement (which, unlike the dupes in Poe's story, we have the illusion of finding). As a corollary we may add that the person who is too aware of his submissive desires (and who lacks, therefore, sufficient "belief" in his own rebellious aggressiveness) will not command an easy and natural verbal irony, since such irony depends on the ironist's ability to consciously identify himself with only *one* of the two warring impulses within him.

The argument we have just made can be summarized as two points. First, verbal irony has its roots in the same kind of ambivalence, with basically the same conflicting impulses, that gives rise to obsessive-compulsive neurosis. There is, however, a significant difference in the relative strengths of the two impulses and in the balance these impulses can achieve—hence the very different outcomes to which the fundamental ambivalence leads in the obsessive neurotic and in the ironist. Second, both *Gulliver's Travels* and *The Trial* symbolically reenact the origin of this kind of ambivalence when they portray the intrusion of the demands of authority into the most fundamental instinctual gratification, that of eating. We may add that, a bit later in each book, authority completely forbids the other fundamental instinct, the sexual one, from achieving any gratification. We have already analyzed at length the oedipal plot that comes to dominate the "Voyage to

Lilliput," and a similar plot also lies behind the action of *The Trial*, centering of course on the figure of Fräulein Bürstner. One need only think, for example, of the incident at the end of the second chapter (in Pasley's new critical edition; chap. 1 in the English translation): K. has forced himself upon Fräulein Bürstner and is kissing her passionately on the neck, when loud knocking from the next room—the protest of Captain Lanz, who has just started sleeping there—forces K. to end his seduction and return to his own room. K. is never given another opportunity to get near Fräulein Bürstner. There is, however, a significant difference between the oedipal plots of the two novels—one that will help us see why irony makes a much more striking appearance in *Gulliver's Travels*—and we will return to this difference after looking at one final similarity.

If authority in both books must be hated for contaminating the two most important instinctual gratifications, nonetheless both Gulliver and Josef K. exhibit tremendous unconscious fear of openly attacking this authority. Again, we have already shown in detail how Gulliver, in his infantile megalomania, believes himself stronger and more powerful than the Lilliputians. Yet even though the book gives substance to this fantasy, Gulliver still refuses to actually test his strength against the Lilliputians or their emperor, all the while offering himself various lame excuses for not doing so. In *The Trial* we find exactly the same psychological mechanism operating in Josef K., and, as with Gulliver, it appears most clearly just after the opening "arrest." Here is an example of K.'s thinking in the first chapter:

> Vielleicht würden ihn die Beiden [Wächter], wenn er die Tür des folgenden Zimmers oder gar die Tür des Vorzimmers öffnen würde, gar nicht zu hindern wagen, vielleicht wäre es die einfachste Lösung des Ganzen, daß er es auf die Spitze trieb. Aber vielleicht würden sie ihn doch packen und war er einmal niedergeworfen, so war auch alle Überlegenheit verloren, die er ihnen jetzt gegenüber in gewisser Hinsicht doch wahrte. Deshalb zog er die Sicherheit der Lösung vor, wie sie der natürliche Verlauf bringen mußte, und ging in sein Zimmer zurück. (16)
>
> [If he were to open the door of the next room or even the door leading to the hall, perhaps the two of them (i.e., the warders) would not dare to hinder him, perhaps that would be the simplest solution of the whole business, to bring it to a head. But perhaps they might seize him after all, and if he were once

down, all the superiority would be lost which in a certain sense
he still retained. Accordingly, instead of a quick solution he
chose that certainty which the natural course of things would be
bound to bring, and went back to his room. (7–8)]

There is much feisty rebelliousness in both *Gulliver's Travels* and
The Trial, but there is also very little in the way of a direct, open
attack against the authorities who have forbidden Gulliver and K.
the gratifications they crave. Indeed, the plot curves of the two
books show a development *away* from such aggressiveness: Gulliver and K. both end up trying to repress all rebelliousness and to
perfect their identification with the oppressive authorities. This
movement is absolutely explicit in *The Trial*, of course, when
Josef K. almost succeeds in identifying himself with the judgment
of the court. Thus, when the two executioners show up at K.'s
apartment, he has already anticipated their arrival and is dressed
and ready to leave calmly with them. The rest of the chapter
details K.'s attempt to embrace the verdict of the court and to
make it his own. As the two executioners pass the knife back and
forth over him, K. even realizes that it is his duty to seize the knife
and plunge it into his own breast. But he cannot force himself to
take this final step, and hence the total identification with the
authorities (and with his own superego) that he so greatly desires
is denied him. This identification seems to him the only possible
escape from the terrible ambivalence that has been tearing him
apart, for the path of rebellion has seemed even more frightening
and more unbearable than the path of identification, even though
the latter leads to the severe punishment to which he is now subject. On the other hand, the fact that this inhuman identification,
however wished for and sought after, cannot be consummated is
the faint light of salvation that remains unextinguished at the end
of the novel.[1]

The same desperate wish to dissolve the pain of rebellious
ambivalence by moving into a state of total identification is
played out as well in the last part of *Gulliver's Travels*, the "Voyage to the Country of the Houyhnhnms." Here the underlying
psychological aim is much better hidden than it is in *The Trial*.
The emperor of Lilliput has metamorphosed several times in the
course of the book, and he now appears as the benevolent Houyhnhnm sage whom Gulliver calls "my master"—an apparently
worthy model for identification, unlike the faceless higher author-

ities who hand down laws and verdicts in *The Trial*. But what we are seeing, in the person of Gulliver's master and in the other Houyhnhnms, is the fantasy made flesh. Just as Gulliver's "infantile" belief in his own grandiosity vis-à-vis the adult world is made into a novelistic fact in part 1, where Gulliver is portrayed as an actual giant in relation to the Lilliputians, so too, in part 4, Gulliver's desire to identify with the powerful adults and to end his frightening revolt against their authority encounters the only possible set of factual circumstances that could allow this desire to be realized. Gulliver cannot, after all, identify with just anyone. Certainly the *impulse* to identify has been associated with Gulliver throughout the novel, but it has never really won through; at the level of the character Gulliver, there has always remained his unassimilable Englishness among the foreigners (or conversely, his wish to go to sea when he is in England), and at the level of the book as a whole, the ironic undercurrents have represented all along a dissent from identification, undoubtedly, in fact, Swift's own dissent. But now, in part 4, Gulliver is allowed to meet someone so ideal that the book itself seems to endorse Gulliver's wish to identify. This is the fantasy that has been made into a novelistic fact, and, as we did in our analysis of the "Voyage to Lilliput," we must read the "fact" as if it were actually a fantasy.

If we do so, then we see that the Houyhnhnms represent authority as a kind of benign superego—a superego, that is, purged of all the sadism and cruelty that psychoanalysis has found in the unconscious superego and also of all the arbitrary, apparently baseless laws by which the superego governs. What is left, of course, is the ideal of reason. But there is a second, much stranger aspect of the fantasy that is also mixed in. When the child feels that the adult is forbidding him the gratification of his instinctual desires, the child is not simply thwarted but is also envious of the adult who, he believes, is obtaining the very satisfactions of which the child feels deprived. However, Swift's ideal adults, the Houyhnhnms, do not incite this kind of envy, for they scarcely allow instinctual gratifications even for themselves. Their food, for example, consists of oats and hay, and eros hardly seems a presence in Houyhnhnmland. They seem to engage in sexual relations only for the "rational" purpose of procreation, not out of any urge to satisfy the sexual instinct. From the child's point of view the Houyhnhnms are, for once, adults without hypocrisy. They represent human beings who act in accordance with the dictates of a benevolent superego. Of course, the Houyhnhnms do impose the demands and dictates of their own superego on their child Gulliver, but since these commands seem determined by some suprapersonal ideal and are not imposed by an arbitrary parent, then *these* parental (and by extension, superego) demands can be accepted without murmur. *These* parental authorities can be totally identified with.

Or so the fantasy goes. In fact, however, this identification is undermined even as it is willed. No matter how benevolent or how reasonable, the authority of the parent and later of the super-ego is still opposed to the gratification of the instincts and there-fore cannot simply be submitted to without further ado. Thus, Swift's irony touches even the Houyhnhnms, as many readers have felt and as we have shown in detail in chapter 2. And at the end of the book, Gulliver's identification with the Houyhnhnms becomes itself the subject of biting irony. The fantasy of identifi-cation must have belonged to Swift as well as to Gulliver (for with the exception of some significant, but rather subdued irony, the fantasy is presented with the author's conviction), but as I have tried to show, it is the desire for identification that the ironist typ-ically represses.[2] Therefore, the last moment of Swift's ambivalent to and fro must be unequivocal and must break Swift's own con-nection to the identification fantasy. He achieves this aim with his final ridicule of Gulliver's attempts to ape the Houyhnhnms.

We see, then, that both books move toward an incompletely realized enactment of an identification with authority. To be sure, by disavowing the wish behind this movement of the plot, Swift maintains the ironist's typical posture—that is, an incomplete awareness of one half of his ambivalent attitude toward authority (the ambivalence being, nonetheless, quite well revealed by an analysis of the verbal irony he uses). Yet the very fact that the plot—the "soul" of the tragedy, and of the tragedian too, we may add—moves toward identification rather than rebellion shows where the strongest pull and also the gravest danger arise. Quite naturally, the impulse that represents the gravest danger—the threat of losing oneself to a total identification with only *part* of oneself, the demands of the superego—is the one that must be repressed if at all possible. Equally naturally, the countervailing impulse, though it has its own dangers as well, is the one that must be strengthened and developed and even flaunted, as proof that the opposite, more dangerous wishes do not exist. So it is the rebelliousness that is allowed to emerge most clearly at the conscious level of Swift's novel and of his irony. This psychological state of affairs is typical of verbal irony in general.

In *The Trial*, Kafka's attitude toward the desired identification seems quite different. Any effacing of one's own ego on account of a massive identification with authority is, of course, self-damaging and masochistic, but Swift obscures this aspect of the wish for identification by idealizing the objects of that wish. Kafka, on the other hand, emphasizes the masochism of his desires, a masochism that is, moreover, not just Freud's "moral masochism" but actually a deeply erotic masochism as well. In Kafka's fantasy, the consummation of his identification is to be achieved at the very moment of his execution, when the father's knife penetrates his breast. The desire for this sexual surrender, which is also Kafka's surrender to the punishing superego, is resisted, but it can scarcely be repressed. For Swift, the erotic and masochistic elements of his desire for identification are so frightening and so deeply repressed that they are in no way allowed near consciousness; therefore, flight from the ambivalently desired identification dominates Swift's expression of his ambivalence, both at the level of plot and at the level of his ironic expression. But for Kafka, the identification, though feared, is also overtly sexualized and becomes a not particularly well disguised goal of his erotic strivings. Thus Kafka's interest in identification is simply too insistent to be effaced in the way that the literal level of irony, the level of identification, must be effaced in the ordinary workings of verbal irony.

In trying to show how fundamentally similar the psychological underpinnings of *Gulliver's Travels* and *The Trial* are, we mentioned that there was nonetheless one important divergence in the oedipal plots of the two novels. A brief analysis of this divergence will now help us summarize perhaps the most significant way in which *The Trial* lacks some of the necessary psychological "prerequisites" for irony that are to be found in *Gulliver's Travels*.

When Gulliver incurs the wrath of the emperor for urinating on the fire in the empress's apartments, he never loses his sense of aggrieved innocence, despite the fact that he has knowingly broken one of the laws of the realm. Gulliver's rationalizations prevent him from feeling any kind of conscious guilt. Indeed, the rationalizations are so effective that we as readers scarcely judge Gulliver differently from the way he judges himself. Whatever oedipal guilt Gulliver may be feeling is buried out of all reach, so that when Gulliver is attacked and punished, he may in full justice try to counterattack, or at least to escape.

In *The Trial*, on the other hand, Josef K.'s sexual attack on Fräulein Bürstner scarcely leaves its perpetrator so untouched by guilt. K.'s sexual impulses are portrayed as the dangerously uncontrolled, even murderous, strivings of an animal, with Fräulein Bürstner as their helpless victim. Here is the description of the kiss with which K. surprises Fräulein Bürstner as she is trying to get him out of her room:

> [K.] faßte sie, küßte sie auf den Mund und dann über das ganze Gesicht, wie ein durstiges Tier mit der Zunge über das endlich gefundene Quellwasser hinjagt. Schließlich küßte er sie auf den Hals, wo die Gurgel ist, und dort ließ er die Lippen lange liegen. (48)
>
> [(K.) seized her, and kissed her first on the lips, then all over the face, like some thirsty animal lapping greedily at a spring of long-sought fresh water. Finally he kissed her on the neck, right on the throat, and kept his lips there for a long time. (29)]

In this brief passage, which represents thoughts that are never far from Josef K.'s consciousness, we see, in fact, the very source of the guilt that drives K.'s year-long trial. To K., his own sexual wishes are so totally fused with unprovoked aggressive and sadistic strivings that to allow these sexual wishes any expression—or, presumably, even to entertain these wishes—is to incur a terrible burden of guilt. The superfluous, and sinister, phrase "wo die Gurgel ist" [right on the throat] shows us exactly how dangerous these wishes actually appear to K.'s unconscious, and the image appears again in the last paragraph of the book, where it clearly links the punishment fantasy with the crime for which the punishment is being exacted:

> Aber an K.'s Gurgel legten sich die Hände des einen Herrn, während der andere das Messer ihm tief ins Herz stieß und zweimal dort drehte. (312)
>
> [But the hands of one of the partners were already at K.'s throat, while the other thrust the knife deep into his heart and turned it there twice. (229)]

K.'s attitude, of course, belongs to Kafka himself; as John S. White notes, for example, Kafka often portrays sexual intercourse as "a sadistic, savage struggle" (in White's phrase) both in his diaries and in a fictional work like *The Castle*.[3]

This sense on Kafka's (and consequently K.'s) part that sexual wishes are also sadistic wishes to destroy the desired object probably has roots that predate the oedipal period. And in fact we can see these preoedipal roots quite clearly in the opening pages of *The Trial* if we recall again that the event that actually opens K.'s trial is his irritation at Frau Grubach's cook for not bringing his breakfast at the accustomed hour.[4] K.'s anger can easily be referred to the child's anger at his mother for not feeding him precisely when he wants to be fed; but for the child, anger directed at the mother is felt as exceptionally dangerous, since the child is absolutely dependent on the mother and cannot afford to provoke her retaliation by his own display of rage. The child's protection in this instance is actually the sense of fear and guilt he develops in response to his anger, since these feelings help him to keep his anger under control, or at least hidden. So we find that, long before the conflicts of ambivalence occur that are generated by the child's struggle against the parents' authoritarian education or even later by the threat of oedipal punishment, the child may have to deal with an ambivalent attitude toward the nourishing mother herself. And what is so important for our understanding of Kafka is the fact that this earliest type of ambivalence is bound to have an essentially different character from the kinds of ambivalence generated later.

Let us try to define this difference. When the older child rebels against the parents' instructions, but also fears to make her rebellion too overt or too extreme, she is likely to be able to tolerate, more or less, the splitting that has taken place within herself and that has resulted in two conflicting wishes, the wish to be the good, obedient child and the wish not to submit to her parents' demands. At this point, she begins to learn out of necessity one or more difficult patterns of behavior to deal with the consequences of this split: She will learn a pattern involving a temporal alternation between her conflicting wishes (such as disobedience followed by pleas for forgiveness)—a predecessor of patterns that may be found in obsessional neurosis; or she may learn patterns that express the conflicting wishes simultaneously, such as rudimentary forms of hypocrisy or casuistry, and these patterns may subsequently include irony as well. Later, in the oedipal period, the child should be able to tolerate her splitting even more successfully, since any wishes that the child believes are forbidden by *one* parent may, again in the eyes of the child, be welcomed or encouraged by the other. If, for example, the little girl wants to have her father to herself, she will certainly feel threatened by the violent jealousy she will attribute to her mother, but on the other hand she will also feel that the father approves of and would reciprocate her erotic strivings. We can see how important this oedipal triangle is to ordinary verbal irony if we recall, from a case history cited in chapter 3, that the child Ernst A., in producing ironic attacks on his father that the father did not understand, believed not only that his mother understood the hidden purport of his remarks but also that she actually approved of her son's ironic attacks.[5] Indeed, we may even hypothesize that this oedipal triangulation is always present in conscious verbal irony—that is, in irony that is meant to be understood by at least some portion of its audience, even though its meaning is formally obscured from everyone. (Obviously some ironic remarks are not consciously intended to deceive any part of their audience.) The psychological roots of verbal irony go back to the child's earliest efforts to resist the parents' domination, but in its ordinary forms, irony always shows this characteristic stamp of the oedipal period. In psychoanalytic theory this connection does not necessarily mean that irony "belongs" to the oedipal period, but let us nonetheless hypothesize that it does—that in irony, conflicts over the wish to identify with and to rebel against a parent's authority, however early in their origin, are shaped just as these conflicts came to be shaped during the oedipal period of the child's life.

We now return, for the purpose of comparison with the later forms of ambivalence that we have just considered, to the earlier form of ambivalence, involving rage against the nourishing mother. At this earlier stage, the child is far less able to deal with his anger toward his mother or with the split in his own wishes. For one thing—and this will be the important point for us here—the child is not yet capable of "inventing" patterns of behavior, such as those we mentioned above, whereby he can act out and externalize the internal conflict. The child cannot externalize (and, therefore, distance himself from) the conflict by giving it expression but must somehow deal with it intrapsychically. And whatever the child does is bound to reflect both the desperateness of the situation and the lack of ego resources for dealing with it. Specifically, if the child uses guilt to control his dangerous rage, the guilt will be overwhelming. If he uses identification with the mother as a way of denying that there are impulses within himself that would sadistically attack the mother, then this identification will be more like an attempt to deny his own individuation than like a more mature identification that preserves some ego identity.

Now, without attempting any kind of exact reconstruction of Kafka's preoedipal biography, let us simply say that almost all the psychological characteristics we have been pointing to in *The Trial* would seem to belong to the primitive extremism of a pre-oedipal state. One obvious example would be the fact that the action of *The Trial* is, in its essence, intrapsychic. Another would be the irreducible sense of guilt, resulting from the belief that all erotic strivings are seen as sadistic and even murderous—a belief that surely reflects the child's ambivalent impulses toward the mother more than it does any kind of later oedipal conflict. Finally, there is the tendency toward that kind of pathological identification that obliterates any sense of self—including the sense that the wishes and judgment of authority might have less than an absolute claim over the self. The plot of *The Trial* is, to be sure, basically an oedipal one, centering as it does on Fräulein Bürstner (or rather, beginning and ending as it does with her). Nevertheless, as psychoanalysis teaches, the *form* of an oedipal conflict can conceal behind it a regression to, or a fixation at, an earlier stage of psychological development. Such seems to be the case with *The Trial*. And indeed, even in the plot there are signs pointing to the underlying preoedipal conflicts. We have already mentioned the fact that K.'s initial anger is due to his not being fed. But we might add that K.'s entire relationship with his mother/landlady Frau Grubach is built around his intense rage at her, rage that he mostly represses but that emerges nonetheless in his coolly sadistic treatment of her attempts at rapprochement, and at other points in the novel. Kafka also imagines a telling reversal in the mother-child relationship, for K. has lent money to Frau Grubach, and she is therefore dependent on *him*.

If we accept that the psychology of *The Trial* fundamentally belongs to the early stages of a troubled relationship with the nourishing mother, then we can see why the oedipal crises in the book are negotiated so badly. K. does not have enough ego strength to resist total identification with the punishing oedipal father. In addition, his guilt is not the ambivalent guilt of the oedi-pal period but a more overwhelming guilt that is used earlier to suppress sadistic impulses against the mother. This guilt was orig-inally meant to suppress all aggressive drives, and it is still strong enough to serve that purpose in the present. The aggression K. must turn on himself.

From all that we have said so far about irony, it is clear why irony would ultimately be incompatible with these preoedipal psychological characteristics. Irony cannot exist if the identification with authority is too great. Nor can it exist—as the case of *Gulliver's Travels* shows clearly—unless the ironist can command belief (ambivalent, to be sure) in his own innocence and in his right to his aggression. However doggedly K. (and Kafka) may try to put on a show of having those beliefs, ultimately the beliefs are altogether lacking in *The Trial*.

We can make a similar point by looking briefly at logic in *The Trial*. As we saw in chapter 1, verbal irony is closely allied with the exercise of hair-splitting logic. The ironist is "protected" from counterattack, because he will always be able to show, through close reading and (sophistic) logical analysis, that in fact he has not launched any kind of attack at all on authority and that moreover he has said exactly what he believes, without concealing his meaning through lies. As W. N. Evans has pointed out, this aspect of verbal irony is related to that kind of casuistry that justifies behavior by appealing in a strict and logical fashion to the letter of the law, while at the same time violating its spirit.[6] Just as the child uses casuistry to circumvent the commands of the parent (and later the adult uses it to get around the superego), so too the ironist appeals to the letter of his own speech to "prove" to the adult that no aggression against the adult was intended. Careful use of logic becomes the guarantor of the ironist's "innocence"— even, or perhaps especially, to the ironist herself. Of course, the ironist's touching faith in logic is a reflection of the imperious superego command to which she herself has become subject during childhood—the command to make sense or, as we might put it in more overtly logical terms, the command to obey the law of contradiction. But it is important to note that the ironist is operating at the particular level of psychological maturity (that of later childhood) at which the authoritarian demands of the parents are being universalized in the superego as laws that are to apply to everyone else as well as to herself. As we have noted, Freud points out how eagerly we escape, if only for a moment, the oppressive weight of the adult command to make sense, as our delight in nonsense jokes demonstrates.[7] But the ironist's rebellion against this and other authoritarian edicts takes a more perverse twist:

the ironist holds the adults to their own law and uses it to attack them or their dicta with impunity.

The same obsession with logic that is implicit in the ironist's verbal behavior, or in the casuist's, may certainly be found in *The Trial* as well. But the difference is significant. Whereas the ironist *assumes* that logic holds as a universal law (which he can therefore take advantage of, as well as be oppressed by), that very assumption becomes an object of inquiry in Kafka's novel. It would seem, moreover, that in the course of his trial K. learns to reject this assumption. In the next-to-last chapter, "Im Dom" [In the Cathedral], K. and the priest subject the famous parable "Vor dem Gesetz" [Before the Law] to a thoroughgoing analysis that involves absolute attention to the literal level of the text combined with careful logical deduction—precisely those two moves by which the ironist (unconsciously) feels that he can prove his remarks empty of aggressive, hostile intent. At the very end of their analysis, however, the priest and K. come to two different conclusions, and when the priest says that to doubt the door-keeper's dignity would be to doubt the law itself, K. demurs:

> "Mit dieser Meinung stimme ich nicht überein," sagte K. kopf-schüttelnd, "denn wenn man sich ihr anschließt, muß man alles was der Türhüter sagt für wahr halten. Daß das aber nicht möglich ist, hast Du ja selbst ausführlich begründet." "Nein," sagte der Geistliche, "man muß nicht alles für wahr halten, man muß es nur für notwendig halten." "Trübselige Meinung," sagte K. "Die Lüge wird zur Weltordnung gemacht." (302–3)
>
> ["I don't agree with that point of view," said K., shaking his head, "for if one accepts it, one must accept as true everything the doorkeeper says. But you yourself have sufficiently proved how impossible it is to do that." "No," said the priest, "it is not necessary to accept everything as true, one must only accept it as necessary." "A melancholy conclusion," said K. "It turns lying into a universal principle." (220)]

We can easily translate K.'s metaphysical conclusion back into a psychological one—namely, that K. has no belief that the power-ful adults will act rationally. And in fact, this lack of faith accords well enough with the passage from Kafka's "Letter to His Father," quoted in chapter 3, in which Kafka accuses his father of not feel-ing bound by the laws of logic, of believing that the *ipse dixit* of authority (what in the *Trial* passage just cited is labeled as the "necessary") was sufficient of itself. Some children, faced with a

similar discovery, will attempt to restore their faith in the rationality of their parents by twisting their *other* beliefs in such a way
that the parents' actions can again be interpreted as rational.
Thus, at the simplest level, the child who feels that he is being
rebuked or punished unjustly will begin to find in himself some
kind of guilt that will justify the otherwise irrational punishment.
This move, of course, is precisely the one that K. attempts to
make when, having attempted to prove throughout the book that
a rational legal authority would judge him innocent, he realizes
(especially in the passage just quoted) that he cannot have both
his own innocence and a rational authority. His subsequent effort
to preserve his belief in the latter leads him to abandon, or to
attempt to abandon, his apparently less important belief in his
own innocence. But what is of course clear from *The Trial* is that
Kafka's instinctive faith in the submission of authority to the laws
of rationality is always tenuous—far too tenuous, in fact, to support verbal irony, which depends, as we have tried to show, on
just that kind of deep-rooted faith.

We may also note in passing that Kafka later expressed a similar lack of faith in the power of negation. In the Fourth Octavo
Notebook (called Octavo Notebook "G" in the new critical edition), Kafka made the following entry for February 4, 1918:

> In einer Welt der Lüge wird die Lüge nicht einmal durch ihren
> Gegensatz aus der Welt geschafft, sondern nur durch eine Welt
> der Wahrheit.
>
> [In a world of lies the lie is not removed from the world by
> means of its opposite, but only by means of a world of truth.][8]

If one statement cannot banish its opposite, then the ironist is in a
precariously exposed position, for the literal level will not recede
before the covert level. Nor will the law of contradiction hold, so
that all of the logical niceties by means of which the ironist
unconsciously protects herself (as we discussed in chap. 1) will
lose whatever screening value they may have had. The unconscious, Freud said, does not know the concept of negation; however, because negation is indispensable to conscious thought, the
unconscious may use it—and presumably its derivatives, of which
irony is surely one—to express forbidden impulses in a disguised
form. But if Kafka has in some sense lost his belief in the power of
the contradictory, then his relation to his own irony will necessarily be troubled.

All the various factors we have just focused on—Kafka's lack of belief in the applicability of reason to authority (and to the superego), his lack of belief in his own innocence, and his lack of belief in his right to aggression—may be related to that strong sense we get in *The Trial* that no real contact is being made with anything outside the consciousness that has dreamed or invented the events of the novel. The claustrophobic battle is being fought out in the interior of this consciousness. How different this feeling is from the one we get from *Gulliver's Travels*, where Swift represents an external world that is just as fantastical (and just as realistic) as the one in *The Trial*, yet where actual contact seems to take place between Gulliver and the world around him and between Swift and the world he has represented. This difference between the two books corresponds roughly to the difference between two neuroses: depression and compulsion neurosis. In *The Psychoanalytic Theory of Neurosis*, Otto Fenichel compares the two neuroses on the basis of a certain, very pronounced underlying similarity. Both neuroses, he says, are characterized by "an ambivalent dependence on a sadistic superego and the necessity to get rid of an unbearable guilt tension at any cost." Since these two factors are the most frequent causes of suicide, we would expect suicide to appear sometimes in the course of both neuroses; but in fact suicide is very rare among compulsive patients. Fenichel says, following Freud, that this unexpected result depends on a crucial difference between the two neuroses:

> In compulsion neurosis, in contrast to depression, the libido of the individual is not totally involved in the conflict between the ego and the superego; a large part of the patient's object relationships is preserved, and this circumstance protects him from ruin; it may even be that the regressive distortion of these remaining object relationships, that is, their sadistic nature, contributes to this favorable effect: because the compulsion neurotic succeeds in actually expressing so much aggression against objects, he does not need to turn so much aggression against himself.[9]

We do not need to make the case here that Swift tended toward obsession and Kafka toward depression. That has, in any event, been done; Phyllis Greenacre speaks of Swift's compulsiveness in her *Swift and Carroll*, and Jules Bemporad explicates Kafka's depressiveness in his essay "Franz Kafka: A Literary Prototype of the Depressive Character."[10] And besides, if we treat these two terms as descriptive of character types more than of well-defined clinical entities, the boundaries between them are hard to pin down. But we want to notice that psychoanalytic theory allows for the case that we have been describing in our comparison of Swift and Kafka—namely, that the two writers, while sharing a certain underlying pathology, did not have the same capacity for venting their aggression toward the outside world even in the relatively "safe" form of verbal irony.

IRONY AS COMPROMISE FORMATION

One of the fundamental insights of Freudian psychology is the idea that most characteristics of our mental life result from compromise. In the Platonic psychology, also tripartite, that is Freud's earliest predecessor, the higher faculties of the mind are there to rule over, to repress and control absolutely, the lower faculties. But Freud saw that this myth of control, persistent as it is in Christianity and Western thought generally, did not explain the facts of human psychology. The recurrent patterns of human thought and behavior, he believed, never represented complete victories by any of the contrary impulses or desires striving for control within a person's psyche. In *An Outline of Psycho-Analysis*, Freud writes:

> Whatever the ego does in its efforts of defence, whether it seeks to disavow a portion of the real external world or whether it seeks to reject an instinctual demand from the internal world, its success is never complete and unqualified. The outcome always lies in two contrary attitudes, of which the defeated, weaker one, no less than the other, leads to psychical complications.[11]

Much of Freudian theory is devoted to showing contrivances by which the "defeated, weaker" attitude nevertheless manages to find expression, and of these contrivances, psychoanalysis describes many as "compromise formations." A compromise formation, such as a neurotic symptom, results when both of the contrary attitudes enter into the makeup of a single characteristic attitude or piece of behavior, such that neither of the contrarieties achieves a fully satisfactory expression, though the part played in the compromise formation by the "defeated, weaker" attitude may remain mysterious and opaque to the actor herself.

This study has attempted to demonstrate that verbal irony is one such compromise formation and to explicate the contrary attitudes that enter into the makeup of this compromise. We started by looking at isolated instances of ordinary verbal irony but then concentrated our attention on the verbal irony that appears, either in a fully developed or in a stunted form, in two of the major works of European literature. In the context of these richly developed, unfailingly truthful novels, we could easily see the full scope of the impulses and attitudes that, in one of their manifestations, led to the irony or the irony manqué that dominates the two works to such a great extent.

Of the two contrary attitudes, no one has ever missed the hostile or rebellious aggressiveness that is usually associated with what we think of as the covert level of an ironic statement. But relatively little attention has been paid to the *literal* level of verbal irony and to the very different attitudes that are revealed there. This oversight is understandable, since in irony it is the literal level that represents the "defeated, weaker" attitude, that is, the attitude that the ironist is trying, somewhat unsuccessfully, to repress. In directing his *own* attention away from the literal level, the ironist keeps the critic from looking too closely as well.

When we do look at the literal level, we find curious things. We find, for example, that there is less contradiction than meets the eye among the various levels of an ironic statement. The ironist unconsciously leaves himself an elaborate avenue of escape, through a thicket of close, logical reading of his own statement, in the event that he is challenged by his victim. His attack is much less bold, and much better defended, than it seems. Even more importantly, we find as we examine the literal level that the ironist is unconsciously expressing his identification with authority at the very moment when he believes himself to be attacking it. But this identification is extremely threatening; for one thing, as the case of Kafka's *Trial* shows, to surrender entirely to this identification would amount to accepting the verdict of own's own sadistic superego and rendering oneself guilty beyond redemption because of impulses and feelings that no human can do away with. Thus, an ironist like Swift (more successful in this regard than Kafka) manages to remain unconscious of the dangerous identification, which finds expression (among other places) only in the "insignificant" literal level of his ironic attacks on authority. And here we have followed up on Bergler's intriguing theory by speculating that the ironist strives to avoid disrupting his view of himself as pugnacious and aggressive as a way of remaining unconscious of his underlying masochistic impulses. Yet these latter impulses, too, are visible in verbal irony, which always involves, to a greater or lesser extent, a symbolic stripping away of the adult powers of the ironist.

So much of the rich meaning of verbal irony is missed when we simply look through the literal level of irony, or study and prize it simply as one rhetorical device among others for expressing a consciously pregiven meaning. Verbal irony is fascinating precisely because so many ambivalent and contradictory meanings are expressed simultaneously and unconsciously under the pressure of an extreme economy of words. Only a perspective that relies on the equally rich insights of psychoanalysis can fully expose the patent and latent meanings of this recurrent form of human expression.

NOTES

CHAPTER 1

1. Sigmund Freud, *Jokes and Their Relation to the Unconscious*, *The Standard Edition of the Complete Psychological Works of Sigmund Freud*, ed. James Strachey, 24 vols. (London: Hogarth, 1966–74) 8: 174. (This set will henceforth be cited as *Standard Edition*.)

2. For the other passage, see *Standard Edition* 8: 73.

3. *Standard Edition* 8: 174.

4. See, for example, *The Interpretation of Dreams*, *Standard Edition* 4: 142–44.

5. Wayne C. Booth, *A Rhetoric of Irony* (Chicago: U of Chicago P, 1974) 176.

6. Roman Jakobson, "Closing Statement: Linguistics and Poetics," *Style in Language*, ed. Thomas A. Sebeok (New York: MIT-Technology P; Wiley, 1960) 353.

7. D. C. Muecke, *The Compass of Irony* (London: Methuen, 1969) 42, 43.

8. Muecke, *Compass of Irony* 232–33.

9. Paolo Valesio, *Novantiqua: Rhetorics as a Contemporary Theory* (Bloomington: Indiana UP, 1980) 113, 105.

10. Group μ (J. Dubois et al.), *A General Rhetoric*, trans. Paul B. Burrell and Edgar M. Slotkin (Baltimore: Johns Hopkins UP, 1981) 148.

11. Paul Ricoeur, *The Rule of Metaphor: Multi-disciplinary Studies of the Creation of Meaning in Language*, trans. Robert Czerny (Toronto: U of Toronto P, 1977) 256. Group μ points out that a version of this idea can be traced at least as far back as I. A. Richards's *The Philosophy of Rhetoric* (*Rhétorique de la poésie* [Paris: Seuil, 1990] 73).

12. Groupe μ, "Ironique et iconique," *Poétique* 36 (Nov. 1978): 427–28 (my translation). The article by Group μ appears in a special issue of *Poétique* devoted to the subject of irony.

13. Dan Sperber and Deirdre Wilson, "Irony and the Use-Mention Distinction," *Radical Pragmatics*, ed. Peter Cole (New York: Academic, 1981) 295–318. References to this article will be given in the text.

14. Cited by Sperber and Wilson on p. 307; the quotation here follows the text of *The Novels of Jane Austen*, ed. R. W. Chapman, vol. 2: *Pride and Prejudice*, 3rd ed. (Oxford: Oxford UP, 1932) 191.

15. For Grice's discussions of irony, see "Logic and Conversation," *Syntax and Semantics*, vol. 3: *Speech Acts*, ed. Peter Cole and Jerry L. Morgan (New York: Academic, 1975) 41–58, and "Further Notes on Logic and Conversation," *Syntax and Semantics*, vol. 9: *Pragmatics*, ed. Peter Cole (New York, Academic, 1978) 113–27. As Sperber and Wilson point out, "Grice's departure from the traditional account of irony is not a radical one" (296), and therefore the details of his theory need not detain us here.

16. For a "test" of Sperber and Wilson's theory, see Julia Jorgensen et al., "Test of the Mention Theory of Irony," *Journal of Experimental Psychology: General* 113 (1984): 112–20. Sperber and Wilson revise their terminology somewhat in their *Relevance: Communication and Cognition* (Cambridge: Harvard UP, 1986) 237–43, but acknowledge that "our account of irony has not substantially changed" (264 n. 25).

17. Catherine Kerbrat-Orecchioni, "Problèmes de l'ironie," *L'Ironie*, Travaux du Centre de Recherches linguistiques et sémiologiques de Lyon (Lyon: PU de Lyon, 1978) 10–46; and "L'Ironie comme trope," *Poétique* 41 (Feb. 1980): 108–27. I have translated the passages from these articles that appear in the following discussion.

18. Kerbat-Orecchioni, "Problèmes de l'ironie" 15.

19. Kerbat-Orecchioni, "Problèmes de l'ironie" 15.

20. Kerbat-Orecchioni, "Ironie comme trope" 109.

21. Kerbat-Orecchioni, "Ironie comme trope" 111.

22. Kerbat-Orecchioni, "Ironie comme trope" 125.

23. Norman Knox, *The Word IRONY and Its Context, 1500–1755* (Durham: Duke UP, 1961) 6, 9–10; and Ernst Behler, *Klassische Ironie, Romantische Ironie, Tragische Ironie: Zum Ursprung dieser Begriffe* (Darmstadt: Wissenschaftliche Buchgesellschaft, 1972) 31–32. For a history of the term *irony,* see also J. A. K. Thomson, *Irony: An Historical Introduction* (Cambridge: Harvard UP, 1927), and G. G. Sedgewick, *Of Irony, Especially in Drama* (Toronto: U of Toronto P, 1935).

24. Quintilian, *Institutio oratoria*, with an English trans. by H. E. Butler, Loeb Classical Library, 4 vols. (Cambridge: Harvard UP, 1920–22) 3: 400–1 (bk. 9.2.44).

25. According to the entries under *irony* and its cognates in such works as *Webster's Third New International Dictionary*, the *Random House Dictionary of the English Language*, and the *Oxford English Dictionary*; Littré's *Dictionnaire de la langue française* and *Le Grand Robert de la langue française* (2nd ed.); the *Brockhaus Enzyklopädie* (17th ed.); and the *Slovar' sovremennogo russkogo jazyka*.

26. Within the rhetorical tradition, probably following Cicero, the word *irony* has sometimes been taken to refer simply to a difference, rather than an opposition, of meanings. Thus, Cicero writes in the *De oratore*: "Urbana etiam dissimulatio est, cum alia dicuntur ac sentias,

non illo genere de quo ante dixi, cum contraria dicas . . . , sed cum toto genere orationis severe ludas, cum aliter sentias ac loquare" [Irony too gives pleasure, when your words differ from your thoughts, not in the way of which I spoke earlier, when you assert exactly the contradictory . . . , but when the whole tenor of your speech shows you to be solemnly jesting, what you think differing continuously from what you say] (*De oratore*, with an English trans. by E. W. Sutton and H. Rackham, Loeb Classical Library, 2 vols. [Cambridge: Harvard UP, 1948] 1: 402–3 [bk. 2.67.269]). One problem with a definition that refers only to a difference is that it scarcely distinguishes irony from allegory, and, as we have said, the rhetorical definition that has come down to us usually insists on some kind of opposition of meanings.

27. Frag. 42, in the *Kritische Friedrich-Schlegel-Ausgabe*, ed. Ernst Behler, vol. 2: *Charakteristiken und Kritiken I (1796–1801)*, ed. Hans Eichner (Munich: Ferdinand Schöningh, 1967) 152. English translation: Friedrich Schlegel, *"Dialogue on Poetry" and Literary Aphorisms*, trans. Ernst Behler and Roman Struc (University Park: Pennsylvania State UP, 1968) 126.

28. Cleanth Brooks, *The Well Wrought Urn* (New York: Harcourt, 1947) 191–92.

29. Søren Kierkegaard, *The Concept of Irony with Continual Reference to Socrates*, ed. and trans. Howard V. Hong and Edna H. Hong (Princeton: Princeton UP, 1989) 65. Further references to this work will be given in the text.

30. For a penetrating discussion of *The Concept of Irony*, see Candace D. Lang, *Irony/Humor: Critical Paradigms* (Baltimore: Johns Hopkins UP, 1988). Lang also offers an excellent overview of current philosophical conceptions of irony, focusing on such writers as Paul de Man and Roland Barthes as well as on the more recent work of Alan Wilde (*Horizons of Assent: Modernism, Postmodernism, and the Ironic Imagination* [Baltimore: Johns Hopkins UP, 1981]) and Gary J. Handwerk (*Irony and Ethics in Narrative: From Schlegel to Lacan* [New Haven: Yale UP, 1985]). Of the last, Lang notes, "I could scarcely agree more with Handwerk's charge that many critics' failure to take into account the philosophical foundations of irony has led them to a woefully inadequate understanding of the phenomenon" (49). I would claim, in contrast to Lang, Handwerk, and others who share their approach, that we can understand irony only by taking into account its *psychological* foundations. See also the critique of Lang in Vaheed K. Ramazani's "Lacan/Flaubert: Towards a Psychopoetics of Irony," *Romanic Review* 80 (1989): 548–59.

31. Jonathan Tittler, "Approximately Irony," *Modern Language Studies* 15.2 (Spring 1985): 32.

32. Muecke, *Compass of Irony*, 19–20.

33. D. C. Muecke, "Analyses de l'ironie," *Poétique* 36 (Nov. 1978): 482 (my translation).

34. Mihail Lermontov, *A Hero of Our Time*, trans. Vladimir Nabokov in collaboration with Dmitri Nabokov (Garden City, N.Y.: Anchor, 1958) 95.

35. Muecke, *Compass of Irony* 34.

36. Freud, *Jokes and Their Relation to the Unconscious*, Standard Edition 8: 97–100.

37. Sigmund Freud, "Three Letters to America," ed. Theodor Reik, *Psychoanalysis: The Journal of Psychoanalytic Psychology* 1 (1952): 5.

38. The English translation appears in Freud, "Three Letters to America" 6, and it has also been printed in Theodor Reik, *The Search Within: The Inner Experience of a Psychoanalyst* (New York: Farrar, 1956) 657. The German text has been published in Theodor Reik, *Dreissig Jahre mit Sigmund Freud* (Munich: Kindler, 1976). However, this volume was not available to me, and so I quote from the manuscript in the Sigmund Freud Collection, located in the Library of Congress, Washington, D.C. I analyze here Reik's English translation, but my remarks would apply equally well to the German original.

39. In *The Interpretation of Dreams*, Freud speaks of "an absurd megalomania [*Grössenwahn*] which had long been suppressed in my waking life" and which he sees as typical of childhood generally (*Standard Edition* 4: 215–16). This megalomania emerges as a disguised element in Freud's analysis of some of his own dreams, and it appears again in the present example, this time as an unconscious belief in an omnipotence that, at the conscious level, he is disavowing.

40. See especially Freud's article "Negation," *Standard Edition* 19: 235–39.

41. Leon Radzinowicz, *A History of English Criminal Law and its Administration from 1750*, vol. 1: *The Movement for Reform, 1750–1833* (New York: Macmillan, 1948) 100–1.

42. No. 61 of *Idea in Sixtie Three Sonnets* (London: 1619), quoted from *The Works of Michael Drayton*, ed. J. William Hebel, corrected ed., 5 vols. (Oxford: Blackwell, 1961) 2: 341.

43. Theodor Reik, "Grenzland des Witzes," *Psychoanalytische Bewegung* 4 (1932): 289–322. This journal was devoted to applied psychoanalysis and was put out by the Internationaler Psychoanalytischer Verlag, the publishing house founded by Freud and his followers in 1919. References to Reik's article will be given in the text; the translations are mine.

44. A cruel Czech captain, who becomes a substitute for the Rat Man's father, tells the Rat Man to repay a sum of money to Lieutenant A. The Rat Man, knowing full well that the money is owing to someone else, has thoughts that Freud interprets as meaning: "Yes! I'll pay back

the money to A. when my father and the lady have children!" (*Notes upon a Case of Obsessional Neurosis, Standard Edition* 10: 218; the lady in question, as the Rat Man also knows, has had her ovaries removed). Immediately afterwards, in punishment for this insult to his father and his lady, the Rat Man becomes obsessed with the impossible task of repaying to A. money that A. never lent him. In my own analysis of irony, I emphasize that self-punishment for the ironic attack is already part of the ironic statement itself. But in obsessional neurosis, the two moments which occur simultaneously in irony now tend to follow one another in time, occasionally in a repetitive pattern of alternation (this point will be discussed in chap. 4). Moreover, whereas in irony the attack is conscious and the self-punishment often unconscious, in obsessional neurosis both moments are generally disguised to consciousness.

45. Reik's point would perhaps serve as a gloss for a comment that Jacques Lacan makes about irony. Lacan says that the "social function" of mental illness is irony. We can see this function clearly in the social relations of schizophrenics, he says; but in the case of neurosis, "irony fails to fulfill its function." Nevertheless, Freud was able to recognize the irony in neurosis, and by doing so, to "restore it to its full rights there— which amounts to a cure of neurosis" ("Réponses à des étudiants en philosophie sur l'objet de la psychanalyse," *Cahiers pour l'analyse* 3 [1966]: 10 [my translation]). I owe this reference to Meredith Skura's *The Literary Use of the Psychoanalytic Process* (New Haven: Yale UP, 1981) 72 n. 39.

46. Chap. 11 of Theodor Reik, *The Secret Self: Psychoanalytic Experience in Life and Literature* (New York: Farrar, 1952) 161–83. This is an expanded version of Reik's earlier article "The Psychology of Irony: A Study on Anatole France," *Complex: The Magazine of Psychoanalysis and Society* 1 (1950): 14–26.

47. Reik, *Secret Self* 165–66.

48. Edmund Bergler, *Laughter and the Sense of Humor* (New York: Intercontinental Medical Book, 1956), and *The Superego: Unconscious Conscience—The Key to the Theory and Therapy of Neurosis* (New York: Grune, 1952). See also Bergler's "Anxiety, 'Feet of Clay,' and Comedy," *American Imago* 6 (1949): 97–109.

49. Bergler, *Laughter and the Sense of Humor* x.

50. Robert Waelder, *Basic Theory of Psychoanalysis* (New York: International Universities P, 1960; New York: Schocken, 1964) 160. Waelder (159) notes that this form of anxiety was mentioned briefly by Freud (*Inhibitions, Symptoms and Anxiety, Standard Edition* 20: 168 n. 1) but discussed in more detail by later writers.

51. Bergler, *Laughter and the Sense of Humor* 188.

52. Bergler, *Superego* 9; italics removed.

53. Bergler, *Superego* 9.

54. *New Yorker* June 29, 1987: 35.

55. Edmund Bergler, "Hypocrisy: Its Implications in Neurosis and Criminal Psychopathology," *Journal of Criminal Psychopathology* 4 (July 1942–Apr. 1943): 605–27. References to this article will be given in the text.

56. W. N. Evans, "The Casuist: A Study in Unconscious Irony," *Psychoanalytic Review* 61 (1974): 397–413. References to this article will be given in the text.

57. For Ramazani's article, see note 30, above; references to this article will be given in the text. Other theoretical discussions of irony from a psychoanalytic point of view include: James Alexander, "De l'ironie," *Revue française de psychanalyse* 33 (1969): 441–50; Rolf Breuer, "Irony, Literature, and Schizophrenia," *New Literary History* 12.1 (Autumn 1980): 107–18; G. Favez, "Le Complexe d'Oedipe et l'ironie," *Revue française de psychanalyse* 31 (1967): 1069–75; David Jaymes, "Under the Sign of Irony: The Use of Paradox in Psychother-apy," *Literature and Medicine* 1 (1982): 80–86; Mark Kanzer, "Gogol— A Study on Wit and Paranoia," *Journal of the American Psychoanalytic Association* 3 (1955): 110–25; Peter Schofer and Donald Rice, "The Rhetoric of Displacement and Condensation," *Pre/Text* 3 (1982): 9–29; Sidney Tarachow, "Ambiguity and Human Imperfection," *Journal of the American Psychoanalytic Association* 13 (1965): 85–101; and Alfred Winterstein, "Contributions to the Problem of Humor," *Psychoanalytic Quarterly* 3 (1934): 303–16. In *The Dynamics of Literary Response* ([New York: Oxford UP, 1968; New York: Columbia UP, 1989] 54) Norman Holland offers the intriguing suggestion that irony is like the defensive strategy of reversal (in the psychoanalytic sense); however, he doesn't develop this idea in any detail.

CHAPTER 2

1. The only attempt I have found in the Swift literature to connect the irony and the child's fantasies in *Gulliver's Travels* is John Traugott's article, "The Yahoo in the Doll's House: *Gulliver's Travels* the Children's Classic," *The Yearbook of English Studies* 14 (1984): 127–50. Traugott focuses especially on children's games and play. For recent psychoana-lytic thinking about fantasy, including the relationship of fantasy to liter-ature, see the helpful discussions printed in the *Journal of the American Psychoanalytic Association* 38 (1990): Harry Trosman, "Transforma-tions of Unconscious Fantasy in Art" 47–59; Sander M. Abend, "Unconscious Fantasies, Structural Theory, and Compromise Forma-tion" 61–73; Morton Shane and Estelle Shane, "Unconscious Fantasy: Developmental and Self-Psychological Considerations" 75–92; and

especially Scott Dowling, "Fantasy Formation: A Child Analyst's Perspective" 93–111.

2. The "official" line about Swift's satiric purposes has, of course, been attacked from other points of view than the present one. Milton Voigt, for example, in criticizing Irvin Ehrenpreis, finds this fault in the official view: "Ehrenpreis' interpretation is an illuminating example of the pitfalls of didacticism. Ehrenpreis asserts that *Gulliver* is held together by Swift's morality: 'Its true coherence,' he says, 'rests on the moral pattern, the chain of values which the author advocates' [*The Personality of Jonathan Swift* (Cambridge: Harvard UP, 1958) 116]. From such a critical base the heavy hand of didacticism will stretch to all corners of the work" (*Swift and the Twentieth Century* [Detroit: Wayne State UP, 1964] 119). And Norman O. Brown cites Ricardo Quintana's book *The Mind and Art of Jonathan Swift* (London: Methuen, 1953) as one "which perfectly illustrates the poverty of criticism designed to domesticate and housebreak the tiger of English literature" (*Life Against Death: The Psychoanalytic Meaning of History* [Middletown, CT: Wesleyan UP, 1959] 180).

A compromise position is taken by Claude Rawson: "When Breton placed Swift at the head of his anthology, as *véritable initiateur* of a black humour emancipated from the 'degrading influence' of satire and moralising, he told a real truth, for Swift has (I believe) a temperamental tendency in this direction. But the tendency is powerfully held in check by conscious moral purposes which harness it to their own use" (*Gulliver and the Gentle Reader: Studies in Swift and Our Time* [London: Routledge, 1973] 35).

3. A good example of the "humanistic" bowdlerization of Swift is the following commentary (about Swift's scatalogical poems) by Louis A. Landa. It perfectly illustrates not only the willful aversion to any kind of psychological insight but also the unquestioning acceptance of highly suspect "humanistic traditions": "But apart from the more uninhibited language he uses, the privilege of any satirist, Swift reflects traditional views in these scatalogical poems. Their staple is woman as the embodiment of vice, her hypocrisy, her deceptiveness, her filthiness beneath a fair exterior . . . [In addition,] the romantic glorification of what, after all, is only flesh and blood, the exaltation of values concerned with the body, exterior beauty—his corrosive attack on this way of thinking has a strong ethical intention such as we find enduringly in homiletic literature . . . [Is] Swift coprophilous, as the psychoanalyst would have it? Or [is he] concerned with a vital and perennial notion about the dual nature of man?" (Louis A. Landa, ed., *"Gulliver's Travels" and Other Writings* [Boston: Houghton, 1960] xxiv).

4. The classic psychoanalytic interpretation of Swift's life is, of course, Phyllis Greenacre's *Swift and Carroll: A Psychoanalytic Study of*

Two Lives (New York: International Universities P, 1955). Her work, like that of other psychoanalysts writing on Swift, has often been attacked for being insufficiently aware of the literariness (and by implication, the autonomy) of a great work of literary art. But her critics, in their conception of the relationship between author and work, have often displayed as much naïveté (though of a different kind) as they accuse Greenacre of; see, for example, Gail Simon Reed, "Dr. Greenacre and Capt. Gulliver: Notes on Conventions of Interpretation and Reading" (*Literature and Psychology* 26 [1976]: 185–90). Whatever "excesses" it may contain (psychoanalytic criticism is always accused of "excesses," as if these were not found just as plentifully in mainstream literary criticism), Greenacre's work delivers some useful insights to anyone who is receptive to them.

5. I. F. Grant Duff, "A One-Sided Sketch of Jonathan Swift," *Psychoanalytic Quarterly* 6 (1937): 243.

6. Jonathan Swift, *Travels into Several Remote Nations of the World: In Four Parts, by Lemuel Gulliver, The Prose Works of Jonathan Swift*, ed. Herbert Davis, 14 vols. (Oxford: Blackwell, 1939–68) 11: 17 (pt. 1, chap. 2). All further references to *Gulliver's Travels* will be given in the text and will be to Davis's edition. References to part and chapter will precede the page reference (to vol. 11). Thus, the present citation would be given as (1.2.17). The full 14-volume set will henceforth be cited as *Prose Works*.

7. Bergler, *Laughter and the Sense of Humor* 53.

8. Bergler, *Laughter and the Sense of Humor* 72.

9. Jorge Luis Borges, "Avatars of the Tortoise," *Labyrinths: Selected Stories and Other Writings*, ed. Donald A. Yates and James E. Irby, augmented ed. (New York: New Directions, 1964) 208.

10. Nikolai Gogol, "The Overcoat," *The Collected Tales and Plays of Nikolai Gogol*, the Constance Garnett translation, ed. and rev. Leonard J. Kent (1964; New York: Farrar, 1978) 587.

11. For a psychoanalytic reading that views these identifications as signs of progressive development on Gulliver's part, see Bernie Selinger, "*Gulliver's Travels*: Swift's Version of Identity Formation," *Mosaic* 17 (1984): 1–16.

12. The oedipal plot of part 1 was first discussed by Freud's disciple Sándor Ferenczi in his insightful (though often derided) "Gulliver Phantasies," *International Journal of Psycho-Analysis* 9 (1928): 283–300. There is also a brief note by Bryan Axtell, "Symbolic Representation of an Unresolved Oedipal Conflict: Gulliver in Lilliput," *Psychology* 4 (1967): 22–23.

13. The question of Gulliver's status as a character is one of the perennial issues of Swift criticism. Though perhaps the dominant trend is to consider Gulliver, ultimately, as a "novelistic" character, there are still those who maintain that "it would be stretching the evidence too far to suggest that Gulliver is a consistent, three-dimensional character. He is

functional—a device used by Swift to make satirical points" (J. A. Downie, *Jonathan Swift: Political Writer* [London: Routledge, 1984] 272). The view of Gulliver as a "novelistic" character has also been challenged from a deconstructionist point of view, for example, by Terry Eagleton ("*Ecriture* and Eighteenth-Century Fiction," *Literature, Society, and the Sociology of Literature: Proceedings of the Conference Held at the University of Essex, July 1976*, ed. Francis Barker et al. [Colchester: University of Essex, 1977] 55–58). And Nigel Wood specifically denies to Gulliver an unconscious (*Swift*, Harvester New Readings [Atlantic Highlands, N.J.: Humanities Press International, 1986] 68–69).

14. Paul de Man, "The Rhetoric of Temporality," *Interpretation: Theory and Practice*, ed. Charles S. Singleton (Baltimore: Johns Hopkins Press, 1969) 173–209. See especially pp. 206–7.

15. Irvin Ehrenpreis, *Swift: The Man, His Works, and the Age*, 3 vols. (Cambridge: Harvard UP, 1962–83) 3: 446.

16. Ehrenpreis, *Swift* 3: 447.

17. F. P. Lock, *The Politics of "Gulliver's Travels"* (Oxford: Clarendon, 1980) 72.

18. Donald Thomas, "Press Prosecutions in the Eighteenth and Nineteenth Centuries," *Library*, 5th ser., 32 (1977): 316. Quoted by Lock, *Politics of "Gulliver's Travels"* 73.

19. Lennard J. Davis, *Factual Fictions: The Origins of the English Novel* (New York: Columbia UP, 1983) 95.

20. Letter of January 8, 1722–23, *The Correspondence of Jonathan Swift*, ed. Harold Williams, 5 vols. (Oxford: Clarendon, 1963–65), vol. 2 (1963; reprinted, with corrections, 1965) 441–42. The Latin phrase, from Horace's *Epistles* 1.11.10, may be translated "and forgetful of my friends and to be forgotten by them."

21. Ehrenpreis, *Swift* 3: 447.

22. This is Davis's account, given in Swift's *Prose Works* 8: xxxviii.

23. Jonathan Swift, *An Enquiry into the Behaviour of the Queen's Last Ministry*, *Prose Works* 8: 134.

24. W. N. Evans, "The Casuist: A Study in Unconscious Irony," discussed in chap. 1; see especially the passage quoted on p. 72 below.

25. Claude Rawson, one of the finest mainstream critics who have written on Swift—and certainly one with exceptional sensitivity to psychological undercurrents—made a similar point some years ago. Speaking of critics who "assume some form of 'diametrical opposition' between putative and real authors," he says, "I suggest that the relationship is at all times more elusive, and that the rigidities of mask-criticism (even in its more sophisticated forms) tend to compartmentalize what needs to remain a more fluid and indistinct interaction." He adds, "Swift's presence remains felt despite the formal self-dissociation" (*Gulliver and the Gentle Reader* 38, 52).

26. *Prose Works* 13: 149 (my translation).

27. Evans, "Casuist" 405.

28. Jonathan Swift, "Thoughts on Religion," *Prose Works* 9: 263.

29. Ehrenpreis, *Swift* 3: 462.

30. Ehrenpreis, *Swift* 3: 459.

31. Claude Rawson, "The Character of Swift's Satire: Reflections on Swift, Johnson, and Human Restlessness," *The Character of Swift's Satire: A Revised Focus*, ed. Claude Rawson (Newark: U of Delaware P, 1983) 30, 58.

32. The debate over Swift's attitude toward the Houyhnhnms has been so extensive that it has inspired a famous typology, proposed by James L. Clifford in his "Gulliver's Fourth Voyage: 'Hard' and 'Soft' Schools of Interpretation" (*Quick Springs of Common Sense: Studies in the Eighteenth Century*, ed. Larry S. Champion [Athens: U of Georgia P, 1974] 33–49). According to the "hard" interpretations, Swift means for us to be dismayed by "the obvious impossibility of a human being ever approaching an ideal life such as that of the horses"; the ending of part 4 is thus "shocking and tragic." According to "soft" interpretations, this ending is comic, "representing Swift's admission that the position taken by Gulliver in trying to emulate the Houyhnhnms was meant to be funny"; Swift was also "ready to satirize those with extended ideals" (James L. Clifford, "Argument and Understanding: Teaching Through Controversy," *Eighteenth-Century Life* 5.3 [Spring 1979]: 2–3). See also Richard H. Rodino's *Swift Studies, 1965–1980: An Annotated Bibliography* (New York: Garland, 1984), where entries pertaining to this debate are classified as "hard school" or "soft school."

33. For example, in the *New Introductory Lectures on Psycho-Analysis*, Freud writes: "From the very beginning, when life takes us under its strict discipline, a resistance stirs within us against the relentlessness and monotony of the laws of thought and against the demands of reality-testing. Reason becomes the enemy which withholds from us so many possibilities of pleasure" (*Standard Edition* 22: 33). See also the discussion in *Jokes and Their Relation to the Unconscious*, *Standard Edition* 8: 126. Freud, of course, is using "reason" (*Vernunft*) in a slightly narrower sense than appears in Swift's eighteenth-century usage of the term; nevertheless, Freud's point remains relevant to a discussion of the Houyhnhnms.

CHAPTER 3

1. For a psychoanalytic approach to Kafka and his work, see especially, Jules Bemporad, "Franz Kafka: A Literary Prototype of the Depressive Character" (chap. 17 of Silvano Arieti and Jules Bemporad,

Severe and Mild Depression: The Psychotherapeutic Approach [New York: Basic, 1978] 394–415); Peter Blos, "Commentary on Franz Kafka's Autobiographical Document of Sonship, *Letter to His Father* . . ." (pt. 2 of Blos's *Son and Father: Before and Beyond the Oedipus Complex* [New York: Free Press, 1985] 61–102); and John S. White, "Psyche and Tuberculosis: The Libido Organization of Franz Kafka," *The Psychoanalytic Study of Society* 4 (1967): 185–251. Erich Fromm's comments in *Man for Himself: An Inquiry into the Psychology of Ethics* (New York: Rinehart, 1967) 167–71, are also worth consulting, as is Charles Bernheimer's analysis of Kafka's relationship to his own writing (*Flaubert and Kafka: Studies in Psychopoetic Structure* [New Haven: Yale UP, 1982]). Among the standard literary critical works on Kafka, Walter H. Sokel, *Franz Kafka: Tragik und Ironie* (Munich: Langen, 1964) offers the most helpful psychoanalytic insights.

2. Franz Kafka, *Der Process*, ed. Malcolm Pasley, 2 vols. (Frankfurt am Main: Fischer, 1990) 1: 7. English translation: *The Trial*, definitive ed., trans. Willa and Edwin Muir, rev. E. M. Butler (New York: Schocken, 1988) 1. Further references to these two editions will be given in the text; all references to Pasley's critical edition will be to vol. 1.

3. The full sentence, from the entry for September 30, 1915, reads: "Roßmann und K., der Schuldlose und der Schuldige, schließlich beide unterschiedslos strafweise umgebracht, der Schuldlose mit leichterer Hand, mehr zur Seite geschoben als niedergeschlagen" [Rossmann and K., the innocent and the guilty, both executed without distinction in the end, the innocent one with a gentler hand, more pushed aside than struck down] (Franz Kafka, *Tagebücher*, ed. Hans-Gerd Koch, Michael Müller, and Malcolm Pasley, 3 vols. [Frankfurt am Main: Fischer, 1990] 1: 757). The English translation, which I have revised for accuracy, may be found in *The Diaries of Franz Kafka: 1914–1923*, ed. Max Brod, trans. Martin Greenberg with the cooperation of Hannah Arendt (New York: Schocken, 1949) 132. Rossmann is the hero of *Amerika*.

4. William Shakespeare, *Julius Caesar*, ed. T. S. Dorsch, Arden Edition (Cambridge: Harvard UP, 1955) 3.2.87–103.

5. Franz Kafka, "Brief an den Vater," *Nachgelassene Schriften und Fragmente*, vol. 2, in 2 pts., ed. Jost Schillemeit (Frankfurt am Main: Fischer, 1992) 2.1.144–45. English translation: "Letter to His Father," *Dearest Father: Stories and Other Writings*, trans. Ernst Kaiser and Eithne Wilkins (New York: Schocken, 1954) 139. Further references to these two editions will be given in the text; all references to Schillemeit's critical edition will be to vol. 2, pt. 1.

6. Peter Blos argues that, for Kafka, "the idealization of the good, namely, the godlike father imago, became established as a lifelong bulwark against regression to the archaic mother" (*Son and Father* 88) and that this idealization "provided the only attainable protection against the imminent

danger of being swept into the chaos and terror of ego disintegration" (87). As a result, "neither internal nor external aggressive and evaluative confrontation with the idealized father imago was within the son's reach" (74). While my own analysis moves in the direction of Blos's conclusion, I think that Kafka quite obviously makes attempts at aggressive confrontation, however ill fated they might be, and that these attempts point to an essential aspect of Kafka's psyche that Blos tends to ignore. The "blighted" irony that I find in the passage under discussion and elsewhere in Kafka would be one such confrontation, though Kafka disavows and draws back from his aggression in the very act of expressing it. And surely *The Trial*, to take one example from Kafka's fiction, represents in part a hostile critique of the Law, that essence of the idealized father.

7. John S. White cites four instances of such claims: letters to Brod of September 16, 1917, and of April 1921; a letter of June 1918, to Oscar Baum; and a 1920 letter to a young woman, M. E. ("Psyche and Tuberculosis" 188–89).

8. For other responses to the charge that psychoanalytic criticism sees literature merely as a symptom of the artist's neurosis, see Robert N. Mollinger's summary in *Psychoanalysis and Literature: An Introduction* (Chicago: Nelson-Hall, 1981) 23–25. A particularly intriguing response is also offered by Leo Bersani, who argues that even the psychoanalytic theory of sublimation does not obviate the charge, since psychoanalysis tends to view sublimation as just another kind of (symptom-producing) repression. Picking up on a neglected strand in Freud's thought, Bersani suggests the need for a new theory of sublimation, according to which the sublimation in the work of art would represent, not repression, but a kind of "objectless jouissance" (*The Culture of Redemption* [Cambridge: Harvard UP, 1990] 43).

9. Anna Freud, *The Ego and the Mechanisms of Defense*, rev. ed., based on the translation by Cecil Baines (New York: International Universities P, 1966) 110, vol. 2 of *The Writings of Anna Freud*.

10. Harold P. Blum, "On Identification and Its Vicissitudes," *International Journal of Psycho-Analysis* 67 (1986): 269. The 1985 Hamburg Congress of the International Psycho-Analytic Association was devoted to the theme "Identification and Its Vicissitudes"; the papers have been published in volume 67 of the *International Journal of Psycho-Analysis*.

11. S. M. Abend and M. S. Porder, "Identification in the Neuroses," *International Journal of Psycho-Analysis* 67 (1986): 203–4.

12. Joseph Sandler with Anna Freud, *The Analysis of Defense: The Ego and the Mechanisms of Defense Revisited* (New York: International Universities P, 1985) 406.

13. Otto Kernberg, "Identification and Its Vicissitudes as Observed in Psychosis," *International Journal of Psycho-Analysis* 67 (1986): 153.

14. Jorge E. García Badaracco, "Identification and Its Vicissitudes in the Psychoses: The Importance of the Concept of the 'Maddening Object,'" *International Journal of Psycho-Analysis* 67 (1986): 139. Despite the alienating nature of these identifications, García Badaracco views them as "a kind of life preserver," since they help to ward off anxiety over the possibility of self-destruction or ego disintegration (139). In this respect, pathological identifications fulfill the function that Peter Blos attributes to Kafka's *idealization* of his father (see note 6 above).

15. García Badaracco says that "the psychotic, not being able to be a person, becomes a character," someone acting out a role ("Identification and Its Vicissitudes in the Psychoses" 140). The character being played is derived from one of the psychotic's pathological identifications.

16. Freud says as much, for example, in the *New Introductory Lectures on Psycho-Analysis, Standard Edition* 22: 15–16.

17. See, for example, Peter Blos's argument about Kafka, summarized in note 6 above.

18. H. Schneider, "Ironie und Abwehr," *Psychotherapy and Psychosomatics* 15 (1967): 332–33 (my translation).

19. In speaking of Gustave Flaubert, another son who was lacerated by a father's irony, Jean-Paul Sartre offers a brilliant analysis of the kind of turning back on the self that, in different terms, I am discussing here: "Standing in front of his full-length mirror, . . . [Flaubert] *plays the role of someone laughing*, hoping that the imitation will be so perfect that it will be indistinguishable from its model . . . What does he want? To laugh, or to become the other who is laughing at him? Both: to see himself as he is seen (therefore, according to him, as he is) and to disarm the laughter by appropriating it . . . It is of course his father's laughter, the laughter of that sarcastic demon whose irony, by derealizing the child's behavior, made him forever an imposter, that is, other than what he claimed to be, without revealing to him what he was" (*The Family Idiot: Gustave Flaubert 1821–1857*, trans. Carol Cosman, 4 vols. to date [Chicago: U of Chicago P, 1981–] 2: 31–32).

20. Franz Kafka, *Briefe an Milena*, ed. Willy Haas (New York: Schocken, 1952) 175. English translation: *Letters to Milena*, trans. Tania and James Stern (New York: Schocken; Farrar, 1953) 159.

21. Ralph R. Greenson, "The Struggle Against Identification," *Journal of the American Psychoanalytic Association* 2 (1954): 200–17.

22. Max Brod, *Franz Kafka: A Biography*, 2nd, enl. ed. (New York: Schocken, 1960) 116. In the German original, the last sentence reads: "Wenn er sagt: Ich werde Ihnen die Wohnung bezahlen—lacht er, als ob es ironisch wäre" (*Franz Kafka: Eine Biographie*, 2nd ed. [New York: Schocken, 1946] 144).

23. Malcolm Pasley, "Kafka's *Der Process*: What the Manuscript Can Tell Us," *Oxford German Studies* 18–19 (1989–90): 109–18.

Pasley discusses the composition of the novel in more detail in vol. 2 of his edition of *Der Prozess*.

24. The German original may be found *Der Prozess*, 3rd ed. (New York: Schocken, 1946) 283, vol. 3 of Franz Kafka, *Gesammelte Schriften*, ed. Max Brod.

25. The masochism may have another motive as well, as is suggested by Margret Schaefer's Kohutian analysis of Kafka ("Beyond Oedipal Narrative: Kafka and Contemporary Psychoanalysis," *Journal of the Kafka Society of America* 11 [1987]: 52–60). Starting from Peter Blos's theory that Kafka could protect himself from ego disintegration only by maintaining his idealization of his father, Schaefer accounts for Kafka's masochism in this way: "the self-abasement reflected in the self as insect image can be seen as an attempt to buttress the greatness of the parental imagos surrounding it: if one experiences oneself as low enough, perhaps then one can maintain the fantasy of the other as great enough—a motive for masochism often obscured behind what seem to be oedipal causes" (57). Applying this argument to irony, one might argue, as Reik does in *The Secret Self* (in the passage quoted on p. 34), that ironists attack what they have idealized; in that case, they may also need to preserve this idealization in some fashion or another and can do so only by simultaneously abasing themselves as they abase the idealized authority.

26. Charles Brenner, "The Masochistic Character: Genesis and Treatment," *Journal of the American Psychoanalytic Association* 7 (1959): 224.

27. On the dangers of reifying methodological assumptions (i.e., assuming their validity beyond the more or less limited purposes for which they were invented), see W. Wolfgang Holdheim, "*Idola Fori Academici*," *Stanford Literature Review* 4 (1987): 7–21.

CHAPTER 4

1. At the conscious level, Kafka himself may not have seen this identification as "inhuman" or K.'s failure to consummate it as a hopeful sign. John P. McGowan suggests as much: "[Kafka] desired to be completely one with the Law. His failure to achieve this identification is inscribed *The Trial* . . . At the point where the actions of the self are totally integrated with the intent of the Law, when what one says and does expresses both oneself and the Law at the same time, the self is entirely innocent" ("*The Trial*: Terminable/Interminable," *Twentieth Century Literature* 26 [1980]: 9–10).

2. Phyllis Greenacre comes to a similar conclusion about Swift: "His negativism, always conspicuous, seemed to become stronger [in the

period after the death of his patron, Sir William Temple, in 1699]. He seemed like one who can only feel himself a person through opposing, the more so as he must thus save himself from the counter demand of his nature, to lose himself completely in another" (*Swift and Carroll* 37).

3. White, "Psyche and Tuberculosis" 198.

4. In his analysis of Kafka's "Letter to His Father," Charles Bernheimer sees "Kafka's own myth of origins" as "his mother's refusal to respond to the child's senseless, instinctual demand for nourishment." "In Klein's view," Bernheimer adds, "such a frustration of the need for oral gratification is likely to cause the child to introject the mother as primarily 'bad' and to harbor intense sadistic fantasies against her, fantasies that are carried over onto the father's 'bad' penis imagined inside her and onto his own penis" (*Flaubert and Kafka* 157).

5. See pp. 120–21 above.

6. Evans, "Casuist" 401–2.

7. See chap. 2, note 33.

8. Kafka, *Nachgelassene Schriften und Fragmente* 2.1.82; translated in *Dearest Father: Stories and Other Writings* 90.

9. Otto Fenichel, *The Psychoanalytic Theory of Neurosis* (New York: Norton, 1945) 294.

10. Greenacre, *Swift and Carroll* 252–54; the reference to Bemporad's essay may be found in chap. 3, note 1.

11. *Standard Edition* 23: 204.

INDEX

F